Instant Vortex Air Fryer Oven Cookbook 2020

Simple, Yummy & Healthy Oven Recipes for Your Whole
Family to Fry, Bake, Grill

By Barbara Emmerich

Legal & Disclaimer
The information contained in this book and its contents is not designed to replace or take the place of any form of medical or professional advice; and is not meant to replace the need for independent medical, financial, legal or other professional advice or services, as may be required. The content and information in this book has been provided for educational and entertainment purposes only.

The content and information contained in this book has been compiled from sources deemed reliable, and it is accurate to the best of the Author's knowledge, information and belief. However, the Author cannot guarantee its accuracy and validity and cannot be held liable for any errors and/or omissions. Further, changes are periodically made to this book as and when needed. Where appropriate and/or necessary, you must consult a professional (including but not limited to your doctor, attorney, financial advisor or such other professional advisor) before using any of the suggested remedies, techniques, or information in this book.

Table of Content

Introduction

What we eat and how we prepare our foods are both important for good health. Take the Instant Vortex air fryer, for example. In this unique kitchen appliance, you can prepare meals that require little or no oil. It is not just healthier, but it is also very tasty. There are so many yummy delicacies to make that you will never go out of choice — breakfasts, salads, sandwiches, soups, stews, meat, fish, and desserts. You can eat larger portions as you consume without guilt.

The Instant Vortex air fryer is a kitchen miracle! It is a 7-in-1 wonder appliance that air fries, bakes, roasts, broils, dehydrates, and reheats. With so many functions, you don't have to get other devices. It saves your kitchen space and money.

Growing up in a family of doctors, I learned the value of good health from a young age. My dad would take me to the market and always buy fresh stuff. My mom loved to cook. She always managed the time, before rushing to work. The weekends were busy, with more exotic foods and sometimes outdoor eating in our little green space.

I learned the value of fresh ingredients — fruits, vegetables, meats, and fish, and cooking the healthy way.

In this book **The Instant Vortex Air Fryer Cooking Champ!** I will show you how you can prepare 100 mouth-watering recipes and eat the healthy way to lead a better life. For each recipe, I will share a detailed list of ingredients and explain step-by-step the making process. It is going to be very easy.

I will also tell you about the many benefits of this wonderful kitchen appliance, its uses, safety tips, and how to clean it easily. Finally, I will share a 21-day good health food plan that I am sure you will find useful.

This book is for everyone who wants to have a smart kitchen, an appliance that saves them cooking time, kitchen space, money, and an appliance that cooks delicious food.
Thank you for downloading this book.
Happy reading!

Chapter 1 – The Instant Vortex Air Fryer Oven

The Vortex is a multi-use countertop appliance from Instant Pot, a leading pressure cooker and multi-cooker manufacturer from the United States. The Instant Vortex Plus is a smart 7-in-1 device that is unlike anything the business has come up with yet. It is a 1,500-watt convection oven that can achieve a maximum temperature of 400° F. It's 7 functions include – air frying, baking, roasting, broiling, dehydrating, and reheat. There is also the 'rotate' option that lets you make your rotisserie chicken.

Finally, with one single appliance, you can achieve so many tasks, which is what makes it a must-have for the modern kitchen. It is only 13 inches in size, so the device takes up little space. The cooking is cleaner, healthier, easier, and quicker.

It cooks by circulating heated air around your food. You can cook air-fried golden meals with almost none, or very little cooking oil, as the appliance replaces oil with super-heated air. And thanks to its 1,500 watts of power, you can cook anything frozen or fresh.

The inside will be tender, while the outside will be crispy and golden. The Instant Vortex Plus traps the juicy moisture inside the crispy coating efficiently.

An air fryer is more versatile than your deep fryer that can do just one thing. With an air fryer, you can cook fried foods like fritters, French fries, and falafels. You can also roast vegetable, chicken, grill a steak, bake potatoes or a pizza, crisp up your veggie chips, or dehydrate fruit.

Features

- 10-quart capacity
- Product weight – 6.6 lbs.
- Size – 13 inches
- Power - 120V to 60Hz, Maximum – 1500 Watts
- 1.2-meter power supply cord, hardwired, grounded polarized plug
- 7 functions – air fry, bake, roast, broil, dehydrate, reheat, and rotate
- Touchscreen function with 14 touch controls
- Customize the temperature and time for manual cooking
- Smart Programs – Saves the last used temperature and time for each mode.
- Accessories – 2 cooking trays, drip pan, rotisserie basket, rotisserie spit and forks, and rotisserie fetch tool
- Brushed stainless steel front
- The transparent tempered glass door can be removed easily for cleanup

- Dishwasher safe
- Warranty – 12 months

Control Panel

The control panel of your Vortex features an LED Display and touch screen controls. The panel is easy to understand and operate. The manual that comes with this appliance also explains the functions.

- **The Display** – It shows the cooking temperature and time, error messages, and reminders
- **Smart Programs** – This controls the cooking temperature and time automatically. Just select a program by touching the respective label. The display will show 'Off', which tells you that the Smart Program is initiated. Your oven will be in Standby mode.

- **Functions** – Separate programs for each of the functions – air fry, roast, broil, bake, reheat, and dehydrate. Remember, for each function, there is a default cooking temperature and time.
- **Adjust Temperature** – There are [+] or [-] signs that will help you make adjustments to the cooking temperature. You will need to touch and hold for making quick adjustments.

- **Adjust Time** – There are [+] or [-] signs here also for adjusting your cooking time. And like the temperature setting, you need to touch and hold for quick adjustments. The Vortex will save your temperature and time adjustments.
- **Start** – Touch this key to begin your cooking.
- **Rotate** – You can touch this key after the cooking has started. Its function is to turn the rotisserie rotation On and Off. Remember, this is only for the Roast and Air Fry functions. You will see the key turning blue when the Rotate function is available.
- **Light** – This key turns your oven light Off or On. The light will automatically turn off after five minutes.
- **Cancel** – The cooking process will be canceled when you touch this key. The display will show Off and your oven will go into the Standby mode.
- **Smart Program Reset** – Touch and hold this key during Standby for 3 seconds to reset. The Smart Program cooking temperature and time will be restored to the default setting.
- **Full Reset** – Touch and hold the Temp and Time [+] signs together for 3 seconds during Standby. This will restore all Smart Program cooking temperatures and times to the default settings.
- **Sound On/Off** – Touch and hold both your Time and Temp [−] signs for 3 seconds during Standby. This toggles the sound Off and On. But remember, you cannot silence the error alerts.

Instant Vortex Functions

The Instant Vortex Air Fryer Oven has 7 functions.

1. Air Frying – It air fries' food quickly and evenly in the 3-quart basket. There are two nonstick cooking trays and slotted baking sheets. There are several modes inside. Frozen chicken nuggets will come out with a moist inside and crispy outside in only 15 minutes. Frozen chicken wings may take 30 minutes. Grease will drip easily to your foil-lined crumb tray, so cleanup is easy.

2. Baking – You can bake sugar cookies, cakes, bread, and a lot more easily with this appliance. The Vortex holds a 9-inch pie or cake pan, an 8x8 inch baking pan, and a 1.5-quart ceramic baking dish comfortably. Make sure that your dish is either square, round, or oval. You can line your trays with parchment paper. Be careful with the baking time.

3. Roasting – You can easily prepare roasted chicken with your Vortex. So you don't have to eat unhealthy food outside. Use its rotisserie spit function to roast the chicken. It will turn out very tender, crispy, and juice in just 50 minutes. The result will be much better than the roasting pan of a conventional oven.

4. Broiling – This function has received many good reviews. It works at 400 degrees F, which may seem low technically for broiling, but you will see that the result will be very good. Broiling is good for burgers and steaks. You can broil beef at 400 degrees. The meat will be cooked evenly. Broiling is easy in the Vortex. All you have to do is set the temperature, time, and then add the food.

5. Dehydrating – The Vortex won't disappoint you. But like most dehydrators, you will have to wait for some time. However, you won't mind the machine working as it works quietly. You can dehydrate sliced kiwis, apricots, and a lot more. Just remember, the dehydrating function works best for small batches.

6. Reheat – You can reheat using this function of your air fryer oven, so it takes away the requirement of a microwave for a lot of people. However, there is a restriction. You cannot adjust the reheat cycle temperature. Reheat is the only function in this appliance where the temperature cannot be adjusted. You can adjust only the time. The Vortex is set to 280 degrees.

7. Rotate – In this mode, the motor will turn on the right side of your oven. This function works for different cooking modes and reduces your cooking time automatically. The chime reminds you to flip or rotate food. It then continues with the cooking cycle.

Instant Vortex Benefits

There are several things I love about the Instant Vortex Air Fryer Oven.

Healthy	You will enjoy the flavors of deep-fried food, but without the unhealthy oil and also without the mess. The food will be tender inside and crispy outside every time. It works by circulating hot air around your food. Finally, you can enjoy delicious food without the guilt. You will also save electricity. This is responsible cooking.
Saves kitchen space	You will get 7 smart programs in one single appliance. This saves you a lot of countertop space.
Save time	Very little or no pre-heating is required, which saves you time. Both the cooking trays can also be used at once, so you can prepare several meals together. Dinner can be prepared in about half the time compared to a conventional oven.
Easy to clean	Very little grease means minimum mess. You can wipe clean its sleek surface. Also, the cooking trays, drip pan, rotisserie spit, rotisserie basket, and forks are all dishwasher safe.
Perfect cooking	Thanks to the One-Step Even-Crisp Technology, the Vortex gives you food that is always tender and juicy inside, and crisp outside. You will love the browned crunchy texture of your deep-fried food.
Smart, reliable	This appliance is from Instant Pot, a business with a lot of credibility. They are known for their smart programing and many successful products.

Pros –

- The Vortex is a smart device with 7 functions and many handy accessories.
- Its control panel is easy to understand and operate.
- It air fries efficiently, especially with a cooking tray.
- The parts are dishwasher safe. Some of them are non-stick.
- Prepares healthy food as very little or no oil is needed.
- Cooks evenly.
- Works quietly.

Cons –

- It fits into the countertop, but the appliance is still larger in size.
- Manufacturer's warranty for 1 year.

Cleanup & Maintenance

Cleanup is really easy. All the accessories – the rotisserie basket and fork, trays, and the racks are dishwasher safe. So your after-dinner routine will be shorter. Open the door and you can wipe clean the inside. Flour and crumbs can get stuck in the door hinge. But that's not a problem because the door can be taken off for wipe cleaning. If you are unsure about removing the door, then see videos. They are available on YouTube.

You can also clean the trays by hand because of the non-stick coating.

There will be many parts to clean, depending on the food you prepared. Remember to unplug your air fryer and cool it to room temperature before cleaning. Also remember not to use any scouring pads, powders, or harsh chemical detergents on any component or parts of the appliance.

Be careful when you are hand cleaning its rotating basket. Don't use a sponge. It is always better to use a brush instead. Be careful about your knuckles. They may scrape against the fryer's metal graded sides.

Cleaning the Cooking Tray

- Don't cover the tray while cooking.
- Or you can apply non-stick cooking spray on the tray before you add food.
- Remove the tray, disassemble, and clean every time after use.
- Make sure that all food debris and grease is removed completely.

The cooking tray is dishwasher safe.

Outer Body and the Air Fry Basket

- Use a damp and soft piece of cloth or sponge. Wipe dry. This will avoid streaking.
- Always air dry completely before you use it.

Make sure to only use a damp cloth.

It will be a good idea to wrap your drip tray in aluminum foil. This will save you time. Just throw the foil away once you are done.

Storing Your Air Fryer

It's best to store the Vortex in a pantry if you have one in the house. Compared to other kitchen gadgets, this appliance is about average in size. But storing it in your countertop won't be a problem at all. Its dimensions are 14.17 L x 13.86 W x 14.96 H.

Safety Tips

Here are some essential safety tips that are always good to keep in mind.

1. Always use your air fryer on a level, non-combustible, and stable surface.
2. Its outer surface can get hot during use. Don't touch it. Wear oven mitts or mini mitts when you are opening the oven door and working with hot components. Allow the gadget to cool down before moving it.
3. Don't put any type of liquid into its cooking chamber. There are electrical components here that can get damaged.
4. Also, don't immerse the plug or power cord in water.
5. Never rinse the device under a tap.
6. Keep it unplugged from the outlet when you are not using it. Also unplug it before removing or adding accessories or parts, and also before cleaning.
7. Don't use the appliance if your plug or cord is damaged. You must inspect it from time to time. Also, avoid using it if the device is damaged in any way.
8. Don't attempt to modify, alter, or repair any component on your own. This can cause a fire or electric shock. The warranty will be void.
9. Never cover the air vents when you are using the air fryer. This may damage the appliance and prevent even cooking.
10. Remember not to overfill your air fryer basket. Food may come in contact with the heating element if you overfill. This can cause a fire.

11. Avoid pouring oil into its cooking chamber.

12. Make sure to always keep a 5-inch space between the appliance and the wall's sides, above, and backside. Keeping it very close is not recommended. Also, avoid keeping it very close to combustible materials like curtains and tablecloths.

13. Be careful while taking out hot accessories from your cooking chamber.

14. Don't insert oversized metal utensils or foods into the cooking chamber.

15. Always press Cancel and unplug the Vortex immediately if you see any black smoke emitting. Open the door only after the smoking has stopped. Clean the device thoroughly.

21-Day Good Health Food Plan

The food you choose to eat plays a key to your health. And not just the food, even the timing, and how much you eat will matter a great deal. No matter what the condition of your health, remember, it's never too late to make positive changes.

Here is a 21-day food plan that can improve your health considerably. I am providing breakfast, lunch, dinner, and dessert recipes that you can prepare in your Instant Vortex air fryer oven. But before that, here are the best food timings to follow.

Food Timings

1. Breakfast at 9 AM
2. Lunch at 1 PM
3. Dinner at 6 PM
4. Snacks at 11 AM, 3 PM, and 8 PM

21-Day Healthy Food Recipes

Breakfast Recipes

1. Baked Oatmeal with Bananas and Berries

Made with – Eggs, bananas, honey, rolled oats, ground cinnamon, baking powder, almond milk, and blueberries.
Prep Time: 15 minutes, **Cook Time:** 30 minutes, **Servings:** 12
Nutrition Info Per Serving: Calories: 114, Fat: 2 g, Carbohydrates: 20 g, Sugar: 5 g, Protein: 4 g, Cholesterol: 31 mg, Fiber: 3 g

2. Zucchini Noodle Bowl

Made with – Sweet potatoes, olive oil, ripe avocado, chopped garlic, zucchini, water, lemon juice, eggs, sea salt, and chopped green onions.
Prep Time: 15 minutes, **Cook Time:** 43 minutes, **Servings:** 2
Nutrition Info Per Serving: Calories: 362, Fat: 18 g, Carbohydrates: 37 g, Sugar: 13 g, Protein: 13 g, Cholesterol: 183 mg, Fiber: 10 g

3. Pumpkin Pancakes

Made with – Pumpkin puree, almond milk, egg whites, vanilla extract, oats, whey protein powder, ground cinnamon and nutmeg, baking powder, and Greek yogurt.
Prep Time: 15 minutes, **Cook Time:** 20 minutes, **Servings:** 2
Nutrition Info Per Serving: Calories: 285, Fat: 1 g, Carbohydrates: 47 g, Sugar: 9 g, Protein: 22 g, Cholesterol: 8 mg, Fiber: 12 g

Lunch Recipes

1. Avocado and Shrimp Lettuce Wraps

Made with – Shredded cole slaw mix, lime juice, honey, chopped cilantro, shrimp (deveined, peeled), cumin, chili powder, garlic powder, cayenne powder, paprika, salt, and olive oil.
Prep Time: 15 minutes, **Cook Time:** 20 minutes, **Servings:** 1
Nutrition Info Per Serving: Calories: 282, Fat: 18 g, Carbohydrates: 16 g, Sugar: 4 g, Protein: 14 g, Cholesterol: 116 mg, Fiber: 10 g

2. Pasta Salad

Made with – Veggie macaroni, baby spinach, red pepper, sliced olives, marinated tomatoes, crumbled feta cheese, and pesto vinaigrette.
Prep Time: 2 hours, **Cook Time:** 10 minutes, **Servings:** 8
Nutrition Info Per Serving: Calories: 469, Fat: 25 g, Carbohydrates: 51 g, Sugar: 7 g, Protein: 10 g, Cholesterol: 8 mg, Fiber: 7 g

3. Turkey Burgers

Made with – Ground turkey, chili powder, cumin, onion and garlic powder, salt, avocados, lime juice, garlic powder, and olive oil.
Prep Time: 10 minutes, **Cook Time:** 20 minutes, **Servings:** 3
Nutrition Info Per Serving: Calories: 321, Fat: 21 g, Carbohydrates: 9 g, Sugar: 0 g, Protein: 24 g, Cholesterol: 80 mg, Fiber: 8 g

Dinner Recipes

1. Crispy Chicken Parmesan

Made with – Skinless and boneless chicken breast strips, mayo, parmesan cheese, paprika, pepper, and salt.
Prep Time: 15 minutes, **Cook Time:** 30 minutes, **Servings:** 4
Nutrition Info Per Serving: Calories: 262, Fat: 14 g, Carbohydrates: 1 g, Sugar: 4 g, Protein: 33 g, Cholesterol: 92 mg

2. Chicken Slow Cooker Soup

Made with – Chicken breast, olive oil, diced onion, chopped and peeled onion, celery, minced garlic, brown rice flour, chicken stock, Greek yogurt, peas, corn, jicama, pepper, and Italian seasoning.
Prep Time: 15 minutes, **Cook Time:** 5-6 hours, **Servings:** 6
Nutrition Info Per Serving: Calories: 261, Fat: 5 g, Carbohydrates: 28 g, Sugar: 7 g, Protein: 26 g, Cholesterol: 50 mg, Fiber: 6 g

3. Crab Cakes with Sweet Potato

Made with – Cooked crab, mashed and cooked sweet potato, red bell pepper, green onion, egg, garlic, chopped parsley, lemon juice, creole seasoning, pepper, bread crumbs, coconut oil.
Prep Time: 10 minutes, **Cook Time:** 15 minutes, **Servings:** 6
Nutrition Info Per Serving: Calories: 229, Fat: 9 g, Carbohydrates: 17 g, Sugar: 3 g, Protein: 15 g, Cholesterol: 84 mg, Fiber: 2 g

<u>Dessert Recipes</u>

1. Blueberry Pudding

Made with – Eggs, almond milk, maple syrup, vanilla extract, nutmeg, sea salt, cubed whole grain bread, blueberries, cooking spray, hot water.
Prep Time: 15 minutes, **Cook Time:** 1 hour, 20 minutes, **Servings:** 8
Nutrition Info Per Serving: Calories: 239, Fat: 7 g, Carbohydrates: 33 g, Sugar: 14 g, Protein: 11 g, Cholesterol: 186 mg, Fiber: 5 g

2. Chocolate Peanut Butter Pie

Made with – Low fat milk, tofu, chocolate scoops, peanut butter, banana, raw honey, whole wheat pie crust.
Prep Time: 10 minutes, **Cook Time:** 1 hour, **Servings:** 12
Nutrition Info Per Serving: Calories: 258, Fat: 14 g, Carbohydrates: 20 g, Sugar: 9 g, Protein: 13 g, Cholesterol: 2 mg, Fiber: 3 g

Chapter 2 – Breakfast and Brunch

Lentils and Poached Eggs

Prep Time: 10 minutes, Cook Time: 10 minutes, Serves: 4

Ingredients:

- 3 bay leaves, dried
- ¾ cup green or brown lentils, rinsed and drained
- 3 tablespoons of extra-virgin olive oil
- 1 tablespoon parsley, chopped
- 3 cups of water
- ½ teaspoon salt
- 1 lemon zest and juice
- 4 cups of baby spinach
- 4 eggs
- 3 cups of water
- ¼ teaspoon black pepper

Instructions:

1. Keep the bay leaves, lentils and 2 cups of water in your pot. Seal the lid and set to 7 minutes.
2. Meantime, whisk together the parsley, oil, lemon juice and zest, and ¼ teaspoon salt in a bowl. Set aside.
3. Apply cooking spray to 4 small dishes and crack an egg into each dish.
4. Release the pressure, remove lid and drain your lentils.
5. Keep lentils in the pot with spinach and some salt, toss to coat well and cover.
6. Add a cup of water and seal the lid to cook for a minute. Release the pressure for 1 minute again, when the valve drops, remove the lid and drain excess water.
7. Run your knife carefully around the outer edges of the eggs.
8. Spoon oil mixture on top of the lentil before serving.

Nutrition Facts Per Serving

Calories 314, Carbohydrates 22g, Total Fat 18g, Cholesterol 185mg, Protein 16g, Fiber 9g, Sugars 2g, Sodium 390mg, Potassium 590mg

French Toast Casserole

Prep Time: 10 minutes, Cook Time: 30 minutes, Serves: 5

Ingredients:

- 8 eggs
- ½ loaf French bread, chunked
- 3 tablespoons granulated sugar
- ¾ cup milk
- 1 teaspoon vanilla extract
- 3 tablespoons light brown sugar
- 2 tablespoons of unsalted butter, cubed and chilled
- 1 teaspoon cinnamon, ground
- ¼ cup maple syrup
- 1-1/2 cups water
- ½ teaspoon salt

Instructions:

1. Apply cooking spray to your pan. Arrange the bread chunks in one layer.
2. Whisk together the milk, eggs, brown sugar, granulated sugar, cinnamon, salt, and vanilla in a bowl to combine well.
3. Now pour the egg mix over the bread and sprinkle butter. Refrigerate.
4. Pour water in your pot and a paper towel on the pan. Cover with foil.
5. Close the lid and cook for 30 minutes. Release pressure for 10 minutes when the timer beeps.
6. Take out the toast casserole with a foil sling then remove the paper towel and foil.
7. Top with maple syrup and serve.

Nutrition Facts Per Serving

Calories 415, Carbohydrates 54g, Total Fat 15g, Protein 16g, Fiber 1g, Sugars 30g, Sodium 650mg

Asian Lettuce Wraps

Prep Time: 10 minutes, Cook Time: 8 minutes, Serves: 4

Ingredients:

- 1 lb. pork, ground
- 2 tablespoons of olive oil
- 1 bunch onion, sliced
- 2 carrots, diced
- 1 cup of soy sauce
- 1 cup Hoisin sauce
- ½ teaspoon red pepper flakes
- 2 teaspoon ginger, minced
- 1 lettuce head
- 8 oz. chestnut can, drained
- ½ cup of water

Instructions:

1. Press the sauté button of your pot. Add the ground pork, oil, onions, and carrots.
2. Cook for 5 minutes, stirring occasionally. Pour water and turn the pot off.
3. Mix the soy sauce, hoisin sauce, red pepper flakes, and ginger in a bowl.
4. Pour the water chestnuts and sauce over your pork without stirring.
5. Close the lid and cook for 2 minutes. Release the pressure naturally and then unlock the lid.
6. Mix the ingredients evenly and serve.

Nutrition Facts Per Serving

Calories 534, Carbohydrates 45g, Total Fat 26g, Protein 30g, Fiber 6g, Sugars 22g, Sodium 4,642mg

Breakfast Frittata

Prep Time: 15 minutes, Cook Time: 20 minutes, Serves: 2

Ingredients:

- 4 eggs, beaten lightly
- 4 oz. sausages, cooked and crumbled
- 1 onion, chopped
- 2 tablespoons of red bell pepper, diced
- ½ cup shredded Cheddar cheese

Instructions:

1. Bring together the cheese, eggs, sausage, onion, and bell pepper in a bowl. Mix well.
2. Preheat your air fryer to 360 degrees F and apply cooking spray lightly.
3. Keep your egg mix in a prepared cake pan. Cook until the frittata has become set.

Nutrition Facts Per Serving

Calories 487, Carbohydrates 3g, Cholesterol 443mg, Total Fat 39g, Protein 31g, Fiber 0.4g, Sodium 694mg, Sugar 1g

Sausage Patties

Prep Time: 5 minutes, Cook Time: 5 minutes, Serves: 4

Ingredients:

- 1 pack sausage patties
- 1 serving cooking spray

Instructions:

1. Preheat your air fryer to 400 degrees F.
2. Keep the sausage patties in a basket. Work in batches if needed.
3. Cook for 3 minutes, turning over, and cook for another 2 minutes.

Nutrition Facts Per Serving

Calories 168, Carbohydrates 1g, Cholesterol 46mg, Total Fat 12g, Protein 14g, Fiber 0g, Sodium 393mg, Sugar 1g

Spinach Lasagna Rolls

Prep Time: 15 minutes, Cook Time: 12 minutes, Serves: 4

Ingredients:

- 15 oz. ricotta cheese
- ½ cup Parmesan cheese
- 1 cup spinach, chopped
- 4 cloves of garlic, minced
- 1 cup of water
- 1 egg, beaten lightly
- 8 cooked lasagna noodles
- 1-1/4 cups of pasta sauce
- ¼ teaspoon black pepper
- ½ teaspoon salt

Instructions:

1. Pour water into your pot.
2. Bring together the spinach, ricotta, garlic, ¼ cup Parmesan, salt, pepper, and egg in a bowl. Mix well.
3. Spread pasta sauce in your pan, and lay the cooked noodles and spread the ricotta filling on top.
4. Roll the noodles lengthwise and keep inside the pan. Spread the remaining sauce over the lasagna rolls and sprinkle the remaining Parmesan cheese.
5. Use foil to cover your pan and lower it into your pot carefully.
6. Close the lid and cook for 12 minutes. Release pressure once done. Unlock the lid and remove the foil.
7. Serve.

Nutrition Facts Per Serving

Calories 483, Carbohydrates 51g, Total Fat 19g, Protein 27g, Fiber 4g, Sodium 936mg, Sugars 4g

Broccoli & Cheddar Quiche

Prep Time: 10 minutes, Cook Time: 40 minutes, Serves: 6

Ingredients:

- 8 eggs
- ½ cup of whole wheat flour
- ½ cup low-fat milk
- 1 cup of water
- 1-1/2 cups Cheddar cheese, shredded
- 1 cup broccoli florets, chopped
- ¼ teaspoon black pepper, ground
- ¼ teaspoon of sea salt

Instructions:

1. Apply cooking spray on a ceramic soufflé dish, and pour water into your pot.
2. Whisk together the milk, eggs, broccoli, flour, a cup of cheese, pepper, and salt in a bowl.
3. Pour this mix into the dish and lower it into the trivet.
4. Lock the lid and cook for 30 minutes.
5. Release pressure naturally for 10 minutes after cooking. Take out the lid and remove your dish.
6. Add the remaining cheese on top of your quiche. Slice into 6 wedges with a knife and serve.

Nutrition Facts Per Serving

Calories 228, Carbohydrates 5g, Total Fat 16g, Protein 16g, Fiber 1g, Sodium 350mg

Banana Bread

Prep Time: 15 minutes, Cook Time: 45 minutes, Serves: 8

Ingredients:

- ¾ cup whole wheat flour
- 2 medium ripe mashed bananas
- 2 large eggs
- 1 teaspoon of Vanilla extract
- ¼ teaspoon Baking soda
- ½ cup granulated sugar

Instructions:

1. Keep parchment paper at the bottom of your pan and spray with cooking spray.
2. Whisk together the baking soda, salt, flour, and cinnamon (optional) in a bowl. Keep it aside.
3. Take another bowl and bring together the eggs, bananas, vanilla, and yogurt (optional) in it.
4. Stir the wet ingredients gently into your flour mix to combine well.
5. Pour your batter into the pan. You can also sprinkle some walnuts.
6. Preheat your air fryer to 310°F and cook until brown.
7. Keep the bread on your wire rack for cooling in the pan. Slice and serve.

Nutrition Facts Per Serving

Calories 240, Carbohydrates 29g, Total Fat 12g, Protein 4g, Fiber 2g, Sodium 184mg, Sugar 17g

Roasted Cauliflower

Prep Time: 10 minutes, Cook Time: 15 minutes, Serves: 2

Ingredients:

- 4 cups of cauliflower florets
- 1 tablespoon peanut oil
- 3 cloves garlic
- ½ teaspoon smoked paprika
- ½ teaspoon of salt

Instructions:

1. Preheat your air fryer to 400 degrees F.
2. Cut the garlic into half and smash using a knife.
3. Keep in a bowl with salt, paprika, and oil and add the cauliflower to coat well.
4. Transfer to your air fryer and cook for 10 minutes, shaking after 5 minutes.
5. Serve and enjoy.

Nutrition Facts Per Serving

Calories 136, Carbohydrates 12g, Cholesterol 0mg, Total Fat 8g, Protein 4g, Fiber 5.3g, Sodium 642mg, Sugar 5g

Sloppy Joes

Prep Time: 5 minutes, Cook Time: 10 minutes, Serves: 8

Ingredients:

- 2 lbs. lean beef, ground
- 1 tablespoon of extra-virgin olive oil
- ½ teaspoon garlic powder
- 1 teaspoon of onion powder
- 16 oz. tomato puree
- 1 teaspoon chili powder
- 2 tablespoons low-sodium soy sauce
- ½ cup ketchup
- 1 tablespoon brown sugar

Instructions:

1. Heat olive oil to your pot. Add the beef and cook for 3 minutes. Break the meat up with a spatula.
2. Whisk in the garlic powder, onion powder, tomato puree, chili powder, soy sauce, brown sugar, and ketchup, stirring to combine well.
3. Lock the lid and cook on High for 10 minutes.
4. Release pressure naturally for 10 minutes. Take out the lid and stir the mixture, making sure it is combined well.
5. Serve with parsley (optional).

Nutrition Facts Per Serving

Calories 232, Carbohydrates 7g, Total Fat 12g, Protein 24g, Fiber 1g, Sodium 400mg

Chapter 3 – Soups and Stews

Baked Potato Soup

Prep Time: 10 minutes, Cook Time: 20 minutes, Serves: 6

Ingredients:

- 4 cups of chicken broth
- 4 bacon slices, cut into cub
- ½ teaspoon black pepper
- 1 teaspoon salt
- 3 lbs. potatoes, peeled
- 4 oz. melted cream cheese
- 2 onions, sliced
- 1 cup cheddar cheese, shredded

Instructions:

1. Cook the bacon pieces in your pot. Drain out the fat and keep them between paper towels
2. Pour the broth into your pot. Add in the sale, pepper, and whole potatoes. Cook for 10 minutes.
3. Release pressure and unlock the lid. Take it off.
4. Blend the broth and potatoes using a potato masher or immersion blender, until smooth.
5. Turn on the pot again. Whisk the cream cheese in and cook for another 10 minutes, stirring occasionally. Mix half of your cooked bacon.
6. Top with onions, cheese, and the remaining bacon before serving.

Nutrition Facts Per Serving

Calories 588, Carbohydrates 49g, Total Fat 36g, Protein 17g, Fiber 5g, Sugar 6g, Sodium 823mg

Chicken Corn Chowder

Prep Time: 20 minutes, Cook Time: 20 minutes, Serves: 10

Ingredients:

- ¾ lbs. potatoes, cut into half-inch pieces
- 2 teaspoons olive oil
- 1 cup celery, chopped
- 1 cup carrot, chopped
- 1 cup onion, chopped
- 4 chicken breasts, boneless and skinless
- 1 teaspoon garlic, minced
- 2 cups of chicken broth, low-sodium
- 3 cups corn, frozen
- 1 teaspoon black pepper
- 1 jar lemon herb sauce
- 2 tablespoons cornstarch
- 1/8 teaspoon nutmeg, ground
- 1 cup of whipping cream

Instructions:

1. Add oil into your pot and heat for 2 minutes. Stir in the potatoes and cook for a minute.
2. Whisk in the onion, celery, garlic, and carrots. Cook for 2 minutes, stirring frequently.
3. Add the corn, chicken, chicken broth, nutmeg, sauce, and pepper. Stir well.
4. Close the lid and lock. Cook for 8 minutes then release the steam and take out the lid.
5. Take out the chicken, keep on a plate and shred using two forks.
6. Mix cornstarch and place in the pot along with the chicken and cream. Cook for 5 minutes, stirring often, or until the chowder is thick.

Nutrition Facts Per Serving

Calories 392, Carbohydrates 30g, Cholesterol 75mg, Total Fat 24g, Protein 14g, Fiber 7g, Sugar 6g, Sodium 340mg

Clam Chowder

Prep Time: 5 minutes, Cook Time: 8 minutes, Serves: 5

Ingredients:

- 2 bay leaves
- 2 cups coconut milk, full fat
- 1 oz. chopped cauliflower
- 1 cup bone broth
- ½ teaspoon kosher salt
- ½ teaspoon black pepper, ground
- 1 cup celery, chopped
- ½ oz. chopped clams
- ¼ oz. onion, sliced
- 1 cup whipping cream

Instructions:

1. Add the bay leaves, coconut milk, cauliflower, bone broth, salt, black pepper, onion, and celery to your pot. Stir well.
2. Cook for 5 minutes. Release pressure naturally once cooked for 3 minutes.
3. Open your pot and use tongs to take out the bay leaves.
4. Stir in the whipping cream and clams, cook for another 3 minutes.
5. Serve and enjoy.

Nutrition Facts Per Serving

Calories 335, Carbohydrates 18g, Total Fat 27g, Protein 5g, Fiber 4g, Sugar 7g

Vegetable Soup

Prep Time: 5 minutes, Cook Time: 10 minutes, Serves: 8

Ingredients:

- 1 chopped celery
- 1 onion, peeled and chopped
- 1 lb. mixed vegetables, beans, peas, corn, and carrots
- 1 potato, chopped
- 1 cup vegetable drink
- 4 cups of vegetable broth
- 1 can tomatoes, diced
- 2 teaspoons of hot sauce
- 1 teaspoon thyme, dried
- 2 bay leaves

Instructions:

1. Add celery and onion to your pot and cook for 4 minutes.
2. Stir in the potato and vegetable broth. And stir using a wooden spoon, making sure nothing sticks at the bottom.
3. Whisk in the bay leaves, mixed vegetables, hot sauce, and thyme. Add pour in the tomatoes with stirring.
4. Cook covered for 5 minutes and Let the pressure release naturally.
5. Open the lid and take out the bay leaf. Stir.

Nutrition Facts Per Serving

Calories 85, Carbohydrates 16g, Total Fat 1g, Protein 3g, Fiber 3g, Sugar 2g, Sodium 605mg

Jerk Chicken Soup

Prep Time: 10 minutes, Cook Time: 25 minutes, Serves: 6

Ingredients:

- 1-1/2 lbs. chicken things, boneless and skinless
- 2 tablespoons vegetable oil
- 1 onion, chopped
- ¼ cup of jerk seasoning
- 1 sweet potato, chopped
- 2 scallions, chopped
- 1 teaspoon garlic, minced
- ½ chopped green pepper
- 1 oz. drained whole kernel corn
- 1 oz. red kidney beans, rinsed and drained
- ½ cup of coconut milk
- 4 cups of chicken broth

Instructions:

1. Wash your chicken thighs. Pat dry.
2. Pour the jerk seasoning on your chicken to combine well.
3. Pour vegetable oil into your pot. Add 2-3 pieces in the pot and cook each side for 2 minutes. Set aside.
4. Add ¼ cup of the chicken broth to your pot. Remove all brown bits from the bottom with a wooden spoon.
5. Add the pepper, onion, and minced garlic and cook while stirring for 3 minutes.
6. Turn off the pot. Then add the red kidney beans, sweet potato, chicken broth, and corn.
7. Add your chicken thighs into the soup, cook covered for 15 minutes. Natural release the pressure once cooked.
8. Open the lid and stir, Sprinkle coconut milk and cilantro over the top to serve.

Nutrition Facts Per Serving

Calories 297, Carbohydrates 4g, Total Fat 21g, Cholesterol 107mg, Protein 23g, Sugar 1g, Sodium 679mg, Potassium 509mg

Hamburger Soup

Prep Time: 15 minutes, Cook Time: 40 minutes, Serves: 8

Ingredients:

- 1 onion, chopped
- 1-1/2 oz. beef, ground
- 1 can tomatoes, diced
- 1 can of beef consommé
- 4 carrots, chopped
- 1 can of condensed tomato soup
- 4 tablespoons pearl barley
- 3 celery stalks, chopped
- 1 bay leaf
- ½ teaspoon thyme, dried

Instructions:

1. Keep onion and beef into your pot, cook for 7 minutes while stirring.
2. Pour in the tomatoes, beef consommé, and tomato paste.
3. Add the celery, carrots, thyme, bay leaf, and barley. Close the lid and lock it.
4. Cook for 30 minutes and release pressure naturally.
5. Once done, serve.

Nutrition Facts Per Serving

Calories 283, Carbohydrates 18g, Total Fat 15g, Cholesterol 52mg, Protein 19g, Sugar 8g, Fiber 3g, Sodium 950mg, Potassium 661mg

Beef Stew

Prep Time: 15 minutes, Cook Time: 40 minutes, Serves: 4

Ingredients:

- 1 tablespoon butter
- 1 tablespoon of olive oil
- 1 onion, diced
- 2 oz. stew meat
- 6 oz. potatoes, cut into large pieces
- 4 carrots, peeled and cut
- 1 cup of beef broth
- 2 tablespoons tapioca pearls
- 1 tablespoon sugar
- 2 tablespoons of tomato paste
- ½ teaspoon salt
- 2 teaspoons of garlic and herb seasoning

Instructions:

1. Keep the beef in your pot and cook for 5 minutes, turning occasionally. Turn off your pot.
2. Add the remaining ingredients, stirring to combine well.
3. Once cooked, naturally release pressure.
4. Stir before serving.

Nutrition Facts Per Serving

Calories 528, Carbohydrates 25g, Total Fat 24g, Cholesterol 148mg, Protein 53g, Sugar 8g, Fiber 4g, Sodium 777mg, Potassium 1328mg

Fisherman's Stew

Prep Time: 20 minutes, Cook Time: 15 minutes, Serves: 4

Ingredients:

- ¼ teaspoon of red pepper flakes
- 1 cup tomatoes, crushed
- 8 shrimps, peeled and deveined
- 1 fillet of sea bass
- 12 mussels, cleaned and debearded
- ½ oz. calamari tentacles and rings
- 2 tablespoons of butter
- 12 clams in the shell, scrubbed
- ½ fennel bulb, cored and sliced
- 2 tablespoons of olive oil
- ½ cup of white wine
- 4 garlic cloves, sliced
- ½ cup parsley, chopped

Instructions:

1. Bring together the red pepper flakes and tomatoes in a bowl, puree until smooth with your immersion blender.
2. Cut the sea bass into 1-1/2 inch chunks and keep the shrimp, mussels, clams, and calamari in separate dishes.
3. Melt olive oil and butter in a pan over medium heat. Add add the garlic and sliced fennel. Cook for 1 minute and stir the white wine in.
4. Let it simmer for 3 minutes. Add stir in the tomato broth and boil for 3 more minutes.
5. Mix in the bass, parsley, calamari, and shrimp, stir well.
6. Add the mussels and clams, cook covered for 6 minutes. The mussel shells and clam should open, and the calamari and shrimp should get opaque.
7. Transfer to serving bowls and enjoy.

Nutrition Facts Per Serving

Calories 437, Carbohydrates 16g, Total Fat 25g, Cholesterol 217mg, Protein 37g, Fiber 2g, Sodium 551mg, Potassium 888mg

Brunswick Stew

Prep Time: 10 minutes, Cook Time: 35 minutes, Serves: 6

Ingredients:

- 2 potatoes, peeled and diced
- 1 can whole tomatoes, peeled
- 1 cup onion, diced
- 2 cups of chicken broth
- ¼ cup of apple cider vinegar
- ¼ cup of Worcestershire sauce
- 1/3 teaspoon red pepper flakes
- 3 tablespoons of ketchup
- ¼ teaspoon of seasoned salt
- 1 chicken breast halves
- ½ oz. baby lima beans
- ½ oz. frozen corn
- 1 dash of thyme, ground
- ½ oz. okra, sliced
- ¾ cup of cooked pork, shredded

Instructions:

1. Bring together the potatoes, tomatoes, onion, chicken broth, vinegar, Worcestershire sauce, red pepper flakes, and ketchup in your pot.
2. Keep the chicken breasts on top and add thyme, black pepper, and salt.
3. Close the lid and cook for 20 minutes. Release pressure naturally then take out the lid.
4. Remove your chicken and cool on a plate
5. Add the okra, lima beans, and corn in the pot, stir well.
6. Take the chicken out and shred meat from the bones.
7. Keep in the pot again and add pork. Seal and cook for 15 minutes then release pressure.
8. Take out the lid, keep warm and serve.

Nutrition Facts Per Serving

Calories 330, Carbohydrates 45g, Total Fat 6g, Cholesterol 49mg, Protein 24g, Sugar 11g, Fiber 7g, Sodium 941mg, Potassium 1017mg

Chapter 4 – Sandwiches and Salads

French Dip Sandwiches

Prep Time: 10 minutes, Cook Time: 1 hour, Serves: 6

Ingredients:

- 2 oz. chuck roast
- 2 tablespoons of olive oil
- 1 can of French onion soup
- 1 sliced onion
- 2 tablespoons of Worcestershire sauce
- 2 cups of beef broth
- 1 teaspoon pepper
- ½ teaspoon salt
- 6 hoagies
- 1 teaspoon of garlic powder
- 6 provolone slices

Instructions:

1. Season your roast with garlic powder, salt, and pepper.
2. Add olive oil into your pot. Sear all sides of the roast when the oil is hot and take out from the pot.
3. Add onions and cook until soft, turn your pot off.
4. Pour into the beef broth and scrape off bits from the pot's bottom.
5. Add Worcestershire sauce, roast, and the onion soup.
6. Cook for 60 minutes and release pressure naturally halfway.
7. Transfer to a plate and shred.
8. Use a strainer to strain off the liquid into a bowl.
9. Add cheese and meat to your buns before serving. You can also toast them.

Nutrition Facts Per Serving

Calories 708, Carbohydrates 36g, Total Fat 44g, Cholesterol 123mg, Protein 42g, Sugar 5g, Fiber 1g, Sodium 1209mg, Potassium 661mg

Italian Beef Sandwiches

Prep Time: 15 minutes, Cook Time: 90 minutes, Serves: 6

Ingredients:

- 3 garlic cloves, minced
- 3 oz. beef chuck roast, trimmed and cut
- 2 teaspoons oregano, dried
- 1 teaspoon of onion powder
- 1 teaspoon basil, dried
- ½ onion, diced
- ½ teaspoon garlic powder
- 1 teaspoon of paprika
- ½ teaspoon of black pepper
- 1 teaspoon salt
- ½ teaspoon of red pepper flakes
- 3 cups of beef broth
- 6 crusty sandwich rolls
- Sliced provolone

Instructions:

1. Bring together all the ingredients in your pot.
2. Release pressure naturally after cooking for an hour.
3. Shred your beef and save the broth in the pot.
4. Apply Provolone on each side of the bun and keep under your broiler. Place beef on the top.
5. Serve the sandwiches with some broth.

Nutrition Facts Per Serving

Calories 589, Carbohydrates 38g, Total Fat 25g, Cholesterol 153mg, Protein 53g, Sugar 4g, Fiber 4g, Sodium 1366mg

BBQ Chicken Sandwich

Prep Time: 5 minutes, Cook Time: 40 minutes, Serves: 10

Ingredients:

- 1 bottle of barbecue sauce
- 1 oz. chicken breasts, boneless and skinless
- ¼ cup of water
- 1 chopped onion

Instructions:

1. Keep chicken in your pot and sprinkle onions and BBQ sauce on top of the chicken.
2. Pour in the water, close the lid and cook for 40 minutes.
3. Release naturally, take out the chicken from its juices and shred.
4. Pour 2 spoonful of juice over your shredded chicken. Add more BBQ sauce if needed.
5. Serve on your hamburger buns.

Nutrition Facts Per Serving

Calories 214, Carbohydrates 1g, Total Fat 6g, Cholesterol 116mg, Protein 39g, Sugar 1g, Fiber 1g, Sodium 212mg, Potassium 687mg

Bacon Chicken Sandwiches

Prep Time: 5 minutes, Cook Time: 20 minutes, Serves: 6

Ingredients:

- 1 cup of chicken broth
- ½ oz. bacon, chopped
- 1 oz. chicken breasts, boneless and skinless
- 1 oz. ranch seasoning
- 1 tablespoon of cornstarch
- 8 oz. cream cheese
- ¼ cup onions, sliced
- ½ cup cheddar cheese, shredded
- 6 hamburger buns

Instructions:

1. Keep the chopped bacon in your pot and cook for 5 minutes.
2. Take them out and keep between paper towels, reserve some away for garnishing.
3. Pour the broth in your pot and deglaze the pot's bottom.
4. Whisk your ranch seasoning into the broth, and add chicken in the pot with the cream cheese on top.
5. Close the lid and cook for 15 minutes. Release pressure naturally once the timer beeps.
6. Take out and shred using a fork.
7. Whisk a teaspoon of cornstarch into the sauce once the chicken removed.
8. Return your bacon and chicken into the pot, mix well to coat.
9. Place the onions, the reserved bacon, and cheddar on top. Serve on your hamburger buns.

Nutrition Facts Per Serving

Calories 555, Carbohydrates 29g, Total Fat 35g, Protein 31g, Sugar 5g, Fiber 1g, Sodium 1052mg

Chapter 5– Fish and Seafood

Fish Sticks

Prep Time: 10 minutes, Cook Time: 5 minutes, Serves: 4

Ingredients:

- 16 oz. fillets of tilapia or cod
- 1 egg
- ¼ cup all-purpose flour
- ¼ cup Parmesan cheese, grated
- 1 teaspoon of paprika
- ½ cup bread crumbs

Instructions:

1. Preheat your air fryer to 400 degrees F.
2. Use paper towels to pat dry your fish and cut into 1 x 3-inch sticks.
3. Keep flour in a dish, beat the egg in another dish and bring together the paprika, cheese, bread crumbs and some pepper in a third dish.
4. Dredge the sticks of fish in flour, and dip them in the egg then the bread crumbs mix to coat well.
5. Apply cooking spray on the air fryer basket and place sticks in it.
6. Spray each fish stick with cooking spray. Cook in the air fryer for 3 minutes, flipping over, and cook for another 2 minutes.

Nutrition Facts Per Serving

Calories 217, Carbohydrates 17g, Cholesterol 92mg, Total Fat 5g, Protein 26g, Fiber 0.7g, Sugar 0g, Sodium 245mg

Blackened Fish Tacos

Prep Time: 15 minutes, Cook Time: 15 minutes, Serves: 4

Ingredients:

- 1 oz. fillets of tilapia
- 1 can black beans, rinsed and drained
- 1 tablespoon olive oil
- 2 corn ears, cut the kernels
- 4 corn tortillas
- ¼ cup blackened seasoning

Instructions:

1. Preheat your oven to 400 degrees F.
2. Bring together the corn, black beans, olive oil and salt in your bowl.
3. Stir gently until the corn and beans are coated evenly. Set aside.
4. Keep the fillets of fish on a work surface and use paper towels to pat dry.
5. Spray each fillet with cooking spray on both sides and sprinkle the blackened seasoning on the top to coat evenly.
6. Keep the fish in your air fryer basket, in one single layer and cook for 2-3 minutes.
7. Flip over and cook for another 2 minutes, then take out and place on a plate.
8. Place the corn and bean mix in the air fryer basket and cook for 8 minutes, stirring after 4 minutes.
9. Keep your fish in the corn tortillas and sprinkle the corn and bean mix on top.

Nutrition Facts Per Serving

Calories 376, Carbohydrates 43g, Cholesterol 42mg, Total Fat 8g, Protein 33g, Sugar 2g, Fiber 11g, Sodium 2210mg

Zesty Fish Fillets

Prep Time: 5 minutes, Cook Time: 10 minutes, Serves: 4

Ingredients:

- 4 fillets of salmon or tilapia
- 2-1/2 teaspoons vegetable oil
- ¾ cups crushed cornflakes or bread crumbs
- 2 eggs, beaten
- 1 packet dry dressing mix

Instructions:

1. Preheat the air fryer to 385 °F.
2. Mix the dressing mix and the breadcrumbs.
3. Pour the oil, and stir until crumbly and loose.
4. Dip your fish fillets into the egg, shaking off the excess. Then dip your fillets into the crumb mix to coat evenly.
5. Transfer to the fryer carefully and cook for 10 minutes. Take out and serve with some lemon wedges if you desire.

Nutrition Facts Per Serving

Calories 382, Carbohydrates 8g, Cholesterol 166mg, Total Fat 22g, Protein 38g, Sodium 220mg, Calcium 50mg

Mahi Mahi with Brown Butter

Prep Time: 5 minutes, Cook Time: 15 minutes, Serves: 4

Ingredients:

- 4 fillets of mahi-mahi
- 2/3 cup of butter
- Ground pepper and salt to taste

Instructions:

1. Preheat your air fryer to 350 degrees F.
2. Season your fillets with pepper and salt, and apply cooking spray on both sides and keep them in the fryer.
3. Cook for 12 minutes until cooked through.
4. Meanwhile melt butter in your saucepan, stir to simmer for 3 minutes.
5. Take out from the heat and transfer to a plate. Drizzle brown butter on top and serve.

Nutrition Facts Per Serving

Calories 596, Carbohydrates 0g, Cholesterol 205mg, Total Fat 52g, Protein 32g, Sugar 0g, Fiber 0g, Sodium 406mg, Potassium 716mg

Air Fryer Cajun Salmon

Prep Time: 10 minutes, Cook Time: 10 minutes, Serves: 2

Ingredients:

- 2 salmon fillets, skin-on
- 1 teaspoon of brown sugar
- 1 tablespoon of Cajun seasoning

Instructions:

1. Preheat your air fryer to 350 degrees F.
2. Rinse and dry your fillets using a paper towel. Apply cooking spray on the fillets.
3. Bring together the brown sugar and Cajun seasoning in a bowl, sprinkle on a plate.
4. Rub fillets' flesh with the seasoning mix on both sides.
5. Keep the salmon fillets with the skin-side down in the air fryer. Apply a little cooking spray and cook for 7 minutes.
6. Take out from the fryer and set aside for 2 minutes. Serve.

Nutrition Facts Per Serving

Calories 354, Carbohydrates 4g, Cholesterol 99mg, Total Fat 22g, Protein 34g, Sugar 2g, Fiber 0g, Sodium 811mg, Potassium 655mg

Sesame-Crusted Cod with Snap Peas

Prep Time: 10 minutes, Cook Time: 20 minutes, Serves: 4

Ingredients:

- 4 fillets of cod
- 3 tablespoons melted butter
- 2 tablespoons of sesame seeds
- 3 garlic cloves, sliced
- ½ oz. snap peas
- 1 orange, cut into wedges
- 1 tablespoon vegetable oil
- ground black pepper and salt to taste

Instructions:

1. Brush vegetable oil on your air fryer basket. Preheat to 400 degrees F.
2. Thaw the fish if frozen and dry using paper towels. Sprinkle pepper and salt lightly.
3. Stir together sesame seeds and butter in a bowl, reserve two tablespoons of your butter mix.
4. Mix the garlic and peas with the remaining butter mix and keep in the fryer.
5. Cook the peas for 10 minutes, take out and keep warm. Cook fish in the meantime.
6. Brush half of the remaining butter mix on your fish. Keep in the fryer and cook for 4 minutes, turning over to brush the remaining butter mix.
7. Cook for 5 more minutes until cooked through.
8. Serve with orange wedges and snap peas.

Nutrition Facts Per Serving

Calories 405, Carbohydrates 23g, Cholesterol 75mg, Total Fat 21g, Protein 31g, Sugar 4g, Fiber 6g, Sodium 202mg, Potassium 680mg

Keto Salmon Cakes with Sriracha

Prep Time: 15 minutes, Cook Time: 10 minutes, Serves: 4

Ingredients:

- 1 tablespoon Sriracha
- ¼ cup of mayonnaise
- 1/3 cup of almond flour
- 1 oz. salmon fillets, skinless, cut into small pieces
- 1-1/2 teaspoons of seafood seasoning
- 1 egg, beaten
- 1 pinch of seafood seasoning
- 1 onion, chopped

Instructions:

1. Whisk together the Sriracha and mayonnaise in a bowl.
2. Place a tablespoon of the Sriracha mayo in a food processor bowl. Refrigerate.
3. Add the egg, almond flour, salmon, onion, and seafood seasoning to the mayo, pulsing for 5 seconds.
4. Line a plate with some wax paper and apply cooking spray on your hands.
5. Form your salmon mix into 8 patties then transfer to a plate and refrigerate.
6. Preheat your fryer to 390 degrees F.
7. Take out the salmon cakes from the refrigerator and apply cooking spray on both sides.
8. Cook for 8 minutes and transfer to a serving plate.
9. Serve with the remaining portion of Sriracha mayo.

Nutrition Facts Per Serving

Calories 377, Carbohydrates 4g, Cholesterol 107mg, Total Fat 29g, Protein 25g, Sugar 1g, Fiber 1g, Sodium 513mg, Potassium 442mg

Lemon Dill Mahi Mahi

Prep Time: 5 minutes, Cook Time: 15 minutes, Serves: 2

Ingredients:

- 2 fillets of Mahi Mahi, thawed
- 2 lemon slices
- 1 tablespoon olive oil
- 1 tablespoon lemon juice
- 1 tablespoon dill, chopped

Instructions:

1. Combine the olive oil and lemon juice in a bowl. Stir.
2. Keep the fish fillets on a parchment paper sheet and brush the lemon juice mix on each side to coat finely. Then season with pepper and salt. Sprinkle chopped dill on top.
3. Keep the fillets of Mahi Mahi in your air fryer basket and cook at 400° F for 12 minutes.
4. Take out and serve immediately.

Nutrition Facts Per Serving

Calories 95, Carbohydrates 2g, Cholesterol 21mg, Total Fat 7g, Protein 6g, Sugar 0.2g, Sodium 319mg

Crumbed Fish

Prep Time: 10 minutes, Cook Time: 12 minutes, Serves: 4

Ingredients:

- 4 flounder fillets
- 1 cup bread crumbs
- 1 egg, beaten
- ¼ cup of vegetable oil
- 1 lemon, sliced

Instructions:

1. Preheat your air fryer to 350 degrees F.
2. Mix oil and bread crumbs in a bowl, stirring until crumbly and loose.
3. Dip your fish fillets into the egg, shaking off any excess.
4. Then dip your fillets into the bread crumb mix to coat evenly.
5. Keep the coated fillets in your preheated fryer gently and cook until cooked through.
6. Add lemon slices for garnishing and serve.

Nutrition Facts Per Serving

Calories 389, Carbohydrates 23g, Cholesterol 107mg, Total Fat 21g, Protein 27g, Fiber 3g, Sodium 309mg, Sugars 2g

Lemon-Garlic Air Fryer Salmon

Prep Time: 10 minutes, Cook Time: 10 minutes, Serves: 2

Ingredients:

- ½ teaspoon garlic, minced
- 1 tablespoon butter, melted
- ¼ teaspoon of lemon-pepper seasoning
- 2 fillets of salmon, center-cut, with skin
- 3 lemon slices, cut in half
- 1/8 teaspoon parsley, dried

Instructions:

1. Bring together the minced garlic and melted butter in a bowl.
2. Rinse the fillets of salmon and dry them using a paper towel. Then brush the butter mix and sprinkle parsley and the lemon-pepper seasoning.
3. Keep the fillets of salmon with the skin side-down in the fryer, and place 3 lemon halves on top of each.
4. Cook in your fryer for 9 minutes and take out. Set aside before serving.

Nutrition Facts Per Serving

Calories 329, Carbohydrates 1g, Cholesterol 108mg, Total Fat 21g, Protein 34g, Sugar 0g Fiber 1g, Sodium 174mg, Potassium 844mg

Spicy Salmon

Prep Time: 5 minutes, Cook Time: 20 minutes, Serves: 6

Ingredients:

- 2 tablespoons of grill seasoning
- ¾ teaspoon cumin, ground
- 1 tablespoon of brown sugar
- ¼ teaspoon cayenne pepper
- ½ teaspoon coriander, ground
- 2 oz. salmon fillets, with skin

Instructions:

1. Preheat your fryer to 330 degrees F.
2. Combine the brown sugar, steak seasoning, coriander, cayenne pepper, and cumin in a bowl. Sprinkle 2 teaspoons of your seasoning mix on each fillet of salmon.
3. Keep the fillets in your fryer and cook the salmon for 18 minutes, or until cooked through.
4. Transfer to a plate, keep warm and serve.

Nutrition Facts Per Serving

Calories 240, Carbohydrates 3g, Cholesterol 84mg, Total Fat 12g, Protein 30g, Sugar 2g Fiber 0g, Sodium 985mg, Potassium 772mg

Grilled Fish Fillet in Pesto Sauce

Prep Time: 10 minutes, Cook Time: 8 minutes, Serves: 2

Ingredients:

- 2 fish fillets, white fish
- 1 tablespoon of olive oil
- 2 cloves of garlic
- 1 bunch basil
- 1 tablespoon Parmesan cheese, grated

Instructions:

1. Heat your air fryer to 375 degrees F.
2. Brush oil on your fish fillets and season with salt and pepper.
3. Keep in your basket and into the fryer, cook for 6 minutes.
4. Keep the basil leaves with the cheese, olive oil, and garlic in your food processor, pulse until it becomes a sauce. Season with salt to taste.
5. Keep fillets on your serving plate. Serve with pesto sauce.

Nutrition Facts Per Serving

Calories 1453, Carbohydrates 3g, Cholesterol 58mg, Total Fat 141g, Protein 43g, Fiber 1g, Sugar 0g, Sodium 1773mg

Lobster Tails with Garlic Butter-Lemon

Prep Time: 10 minutes, Cook Time: 10 minutes, Serves: 2

Ingredients:

- 2 lobster tails
- 1 teaspoon lemon zest
- 4 tablespoons of butter
- 1 garlic clove, grated
- 2 wedges of lemon

Instructions:

1. Butterfly the lobster tails. Use kitchen shears to cut by length through the top shell's center and the meat, cut to the bottom portion of the shells.
2. Spread halves of the tail apart.
3. Keep these tails in the basket of your air fry. The lobster meat should face up.
4. Melt the butter in your saucepan.
5. Add the garlic and lemon zest. Heat for 30 seconds.
6. Transfer two tablespoons of this mix to a bowl.
7. Brush on your lobster tails. Remove the remaining brushed butter.
8. Season with pepper and salt.
9. Cook in your air fryer at 380 degrees F. The lobster meat should turn opaque in about 5 or 7 minutes.
10. Apply the reserved butter over the lobster meat.
11. Serve with lemon wedges.

Nutrition Facts Per Serving

Calories 462, Carbohydrates 3g, Cholesterol 129mg, Total Fat 42g, Protein 18g, Sugar 0g, Fiber 1g, Sodium 590mg

Chapter 6 – Poultry and Meat

Chicken Curry on Edamame and Asparagus

Prep Time: 10 minutes, Cook Time: 10 minutes, Serves: 4

Ingredients:

- 1 teaspoon cumin, ground
- 12 oz. chicken breast, boneless and skinless
- 2 cups of water
- ¼ teaspoon black pepper
- ¼ cup of light mayonnaise
- ¼ cup plain Greek yogurt
- 1-1/2 teaspoons curry powder
- ½ teaspoon salt
- 1 tablespoon sugar
- 2 cups of cut asparagus
- 4 cups of baby kale mix
- 1 cup edamame, shelled and thawed
- ¼ cup green onion or cilantro, chopped
- ½ cup red onion, chopped

Instructions:

1. Sprinkle pepper and cumin over the chicken, cook for 6 minutes. Release pressure naturally and remove the lid to take the chicken out.
2. Keep on your cutting board, shred after 5 minutes and set aside.
3. Whisk together the mayonnaise, yogurt, salt, curt, and sugar in a bowl.
4. Add the edamame and asparagus in the pot, cook for 1 minute.
5. Release pressure and keep the asparagus mix in your colander. Run this under cold water and drain well.
6. Keep equal quantities of your kale mix on 4 plates. Then add the asparagus mixture on top.
7. Mix the onions and chicken to your yogurt mix, tossing to coat well.
8. Spoon equal quantities on each asparagus mixture serving and sprinkle some cilantro.

Nutrition Facts Per Serving

Calories 253, Carbohydrates 17g, Cholesterol 50mg, Total Fat 9g, Protein 26g, Sugar 8g, Fiber 5g, Sodium 470mg, Potassium 660mg

Green Chili Chicken

Prep Time: 15 minutes, Cook Time: 40 minutes, Serves: 8

Ingredients:

- 1 onion, peeled and chopped
- 2 tablespoons of butter, unsalted
- ½ lb. Anaheim peppers, seeded and chopped
- ½ lb. Poblano peppers, seeded and chopped
- 2 jalapeno peppers, seeded and chopped
- ½ lb. tomatillos, husked and quartered
- 1 teaspoon cumin, ground
- 2 cloves of garlic, peeled and minced
- 2 cups of chicken stock
- 6 chicken thighs, with bone and skin
- 3 cans of beans, drained and rinsed
- 1/3 cup cilantro, chopped

Instructions:

1. Melt butter in your pot, add onion and cook for 3 minutes.
2. Add the peppers, jalapeno, and tomatillos and cook for 3 more minutes.
3. Stir in the cumin and garlic to cook for a minute. Then add the stock and chicken thighs.
4. Cover the lid and cook for 30 minutes. Release the pressure after the timer beeps. Remove the lid and stir well.
5. Transfer chicken to your cutting board. Take out the skin and shred.
6. Puree the sauce in your immersion blender, stir in the cilantro, beans, and meat until well combined.

Nutrition Facts Per Serving

Calories 298, Carbohydrates 19g, Total Fat 10g, Protein 33g, Sugar 3g, Fiber 7g, Sodium 154mg

Rice and Chicken

Prep Time: 10 minutes, Cook Time: 15 minutes, Serves: 4

Ingredients:

- ½ teaspoon of onion powder
- 1-1/4 lbs. chicken breasts, boneless and skinless
- ½ cup Cheddar cheese, shredded
- ¾ cup long-grain white rice, uncooked
- 1 can condensed cream of chicken soup
- 1-1/3 cups of chicken broth
- 3 cups of broccoli florets

Instructions:

1. Layer your chicken with rice, onion powder, and half cup cheese in your pot.
2. Pour the broth over cheese and spoon soup on its top.
3. Cook for 6 minutes and release pressure naturally once done.
4. Add the broccoli and stir well. Sprinkle the remaining cheese.
5. Cover and let it stand for 8 minutes.

Nutrition Facts Per Serving

Calories 479, Carbohydrates 37g, Total Fat 19g, Cholesterol 126mg, Protein 40g, Fiber 1g, Sodium 997mg

Moroccan Minted Chicken Wraps

Prep Time: 12 minutes, Cook Time: 15 minutes, Serves: 6

Ingredients:

- 1 teaspoon coriander, ground
- 1 cup of roasted red peppers
- 1 teaspoon of garlic powder
- 1 teaspoon cumin, ground
- ½ teaspoon caraway seeds
- ½ teaspoon chipotle pepper, ground
- ¼ teaspoon salt
- 1 lb. chicken thighs, boneless and skinless
- ½ cup mint, chopped
- ¾ cup plain Greek yogurt
- 6 light flour tortillas
- 1/3 cup red onion, chopped
- 1 lemon, cut into six wedges

Instructions:

1. Combine the coriander, pepper, garlic powder, cumin, caraway, and chipotle in your blender, puree until smooth.
2. Keep chicken thighs in your pot and place the pepper mixture on top.
3. Close the lid and cook for 10 minutes.
4. Release pressure, remove the lid and take out the chicken.
5. Keep the chicken on a cutting board and shred.
6. Boil for 5 minutes, until thicken slightly. Stir in salt and chicken to the sauce.
7. Whisk together the mint, onion, and yogurt in a bowl.
8. Now spoon your yogurt mix on each tortilla evenly and squeeze lemon wedges on each. Pour the chicken mix on top.
9. Fold the tortilla edges and serve.

Nutrition Facts Per Serving

Calories 293, Carbohydrates 23g, Total Fat 9g, Cholesterol 70mg, Protein 20g, Fiber 7g, Sugar 5g, Sodium 460mg, Potassium 360mg

Olive-Brined Turkey Breast

Prep Time: 5 minutes, Cook Time: 20 minutes, Serves: 14

Ingredients:

- 3-1/2 oz. turkey breasts, boneless and skinless
- ½ cup buttermilk
- ¾ cup olive brine
- 2 sprigs of thyme
- 1 rosemary sprig

Instructions:

1. Whisk together the buttermilk and olive brine.
2. Keep the turkey breast in a plastic bag. Pour the buttermilk-brine mix over. Add the thyme sprigs and rosemary. Seal and refrigerate it.
3. Take it out after 8 hours and wait for it to reach room temperature.
4. Preheat your air fryer to 350 degrees F.
5. Cook the turkey breast for 12 minutes, flipping over. Then cook for another 5 minutes until cooked through.

Nutrition Facts Per Serving

Calories 133, Carbohydrates 1g, Cholesterol 82mg, Total Fat 1g, Protein 30g, Sugar 0g, Fiber 1g, Sodium 62mg

Turkey Breasts

Prep Time: 10 minutes, Cook Time: 25 minutes, Serves: 6

Ingredients:

- 2-3/4 oz. turkey breasts, with skin
- 1 tablespoon rosemary, chopped
- 1 teaspoon chive, chopped
- 2 tablespoons of butter, unsalted
- 1 teaspoon garlic, minced

Instructions:

1. Preheat your air fryer to 350 degrees F.
2. Keep the chives, rosemary, garlic, pepper, and salt on your cutting board.
3. Make thin slices of butter and place on the seasonings and herbs, blend well.
4. Pat the herbed butter on both sides. Keep the turkey in the air fryer basket, skin-down side.
5. Fry for 17 minutes, turn the skin-side up to keep frying for 8 more minutes at 165 degrees F.
6. Transfer to a plate and slice before serving.

Nutrition Facts Per Serving

Calories 286, Carbohydrates 0.3g, Cholesterol 86mg, Total Fat 14g, Protein 40g, Sugar 0g, Fiber 0.1g, Sodium 913mg

Nashville Chicken

Prep Time: 20 minutes, Cook Time: 15 minutes, Serves: 8

Ingredients:

- 2 oz. chicken breast, boneless
- 2 tablespoons hot sauce
- ½ cup of olive oil
- 3 large eggs
- 3 cups all-purpose flour
- 1 teaspoon of chili powder
- 1-1/2 cups buttermilk

Instructions:

1. Toss together the chicken, hot sauce, salt, and pepper in a bowl. Combine well.
2. Cover and refrigerate. Then pour flour into your bowl.
3. Whisk the buttermilk and eggs together, and add 1 tablespoon of hot sauce.
4. For dredging your chicken, keep it in the flour first, toss evenly to coat.
5. Dip in your buttermilk mix, then into the flour.
6. Keep them on your baking sheet. Place in the air fryer at 380 degrees F and cook for 10 minutes.
7. For the sauce, whisk the spices and olive oil to combine well.
8. Pour over the fried chicken immediately. Serve.

Nutrition Facts Per Serving

Calories 668, Carbohydrates 44g, Cholesterol 156mg, Total Fat 40g, Protein 33g, Sugar 5g, Fiber 2g, Sodium 847mg

White Chicken Chili

Prep Time: 10 minutes, Cook Time: 10 minutes, Serves: 6

Ingredients:

- 1 red bell pepper, diced
- 1 tablespoon of vegetable oil
- 1 tablespoon chili powder
- 1 cup kernel corn, frozen and thawed
- 2 cans of white cannellini beans
- 12 oz. chicken breast, boneless and skinless
- 1 can condensed cream of chicken soup
- 1 cup of salsa
- 2 onions, sliced
- 5 tablespoons Cheddar cheese, shredded

Instructions:

1. Heat oil in your pot. Add the corn, chili powder, and pepper and cook for 3 minutes, stirring occasionally.
2. Season your chicken with pepper and salt. Layer the salsa, beans, soup, and chicken over your corn mix.
3. Close the lid and cook for 5 minutes.
4. Release the pressure once cooking is done. Take out and shred it.
5. Transfer to the pot. Season and serve with the onions and cheese on top.

Nutrition Facts Per Serving

Calories 336, Carbohydrates 35g, Cholesterol 42mg, Total Fat 12g, Protein 22g, Fiber 8g, Sodium 965mg

Mediterranean Chicken Thighs

Prep Time: 10 minutes, Cook Time: 25 minutes, Serves: 4

Ingredients:

- 1 red onion, chopped
- 1 lb. chicken thigh, boneless and skinless
- ¼ cup Kalamata olives, pitted and sliced
- 16 oz. baby white potatoes, cut
- 1 can roasted red pepper cooking soup
- 2 teaspoons crushed Italian seasoning
- 1 tablespoon lemon juice
- ½ cup chicken stock

Instructions:

1. Season the chicken with pepper and salt.
2. Layer your chicken, potatoes, onion, Italian seasoning, and olives in the pot. Pour stock and soup over your vegetables and chicken.
3. Close the lid and cook for 10 minutes. Release pressure once done.
4. Stir in the lemon juice and prinkle the parsley.
5. Serve.

Nutrition Facts Per Serving

Calories 321, Carbohydrates 28g, Cholesterol 101mg, Total Fat 13g, Protein 23g, Fiber 5g, Sodium 524mg

Asian Deviled Eggs

Prep Time: 15 minutes, Cook Time: 15 minutes, Serves: 12

Ingredients:

- 6 eggs
- 2 tablespoons of mayonnaise
- 1 teaspoon soy sauce, low-sodium
- 1-1/2 teaspoons of sesame oil
- 1 teaspoon Dijon mustard

Instructions:

1. Keep the eggs on the air fryer rack, making sure that there is adequate space between them.
2. Set the temperature to 260 degrees F and cook for 15 minutes.
3. Take out the eggs and keep in an ice water bowl for 10 minutes.
4. Take them out and peel, cut them in half.
5. Scoop out the yolks carefully and place in a food processor.
6. Add the sesame oil, mayonnaise, Dijon mustard, and soy sauce. Process until everything combines well, or until creamy.
7. Fill up your piping bag with this yolk mixture and distribute evenly into the egg whites.
8. Garnish with green onions and sesame seeds (optional).

Nutrition Facts Per Serving

Calories 70, Carbohydrates 1g, Cholesterol 94mg, Total Fat 6g, Protein 3g, Sugar 0g, Fiber 0.1g, Sodium 102mg

Hard-Boiled Eggs

Prep Time: 0 minutes, Cook Time: 5 minutes, Serves: 6

Ingredients:

- 6 eggs, large

Instructions:

1. Keep the eggs on your air fryer's wire rack.
2. Set the temperature to 250 degrees F, take out the eggs once they are done.
3. Place them in a bowl with ice water, peel them off and serve.

Nutrition Facts Per Serving

Calories 91, Carbohydrates 1g, Total Fat 7g, Protein 6g, Sugar 0g, Fiber 0g, Sodium 62mg

Air Fryer Egg Rolls

Prep Time: 10 minutes, Cook Time: 15 minutes, Serves: 16

Ingredients:

- 1 pack of egg roll wrappers
- 2 cups corn, thawed
- 1 can spinach, drained
- 1 can black beans, drained and rinsed
- 1 cup cheddar cheese, shredded

Instructions:

1. Mix the corn, spinach, beans, Cheddar cheese, salt, and pepper in a bowl, used for the filling.
2. Keep an egg roll wrapper, moisten lightly all the edges with your finger.
3. Keep a fourth of the filling at the wrapper's center and fold a corner over the filling. Tuck the sides in to create a roll.
4. Repeat this process with the other wrappers. Apply cooking spray on the egg rolls.
5. Preheat your air fryer at 390 degrees F.
6. Keep your egg rolls in its basket and fry for 7 minutes. Flip and cook for another 4 minutes.

Nutrition Facts Per Serving

Calories 260, Carbohydrates 27g, Cholesterol 25mg, Total Fat 12g, Protein 11g, Sugar 1g, Fiber 4g, Sodium 628mg

Scotch Eggs

Prep Time: 15 minutes, Cook Time: 15 minutes, Serves: 6

Ingredients:

- 2 tablespoons of mango chutney
- 3 tablespoons of Greek yogurt
- 1/8 teaspoon pepper
- 1/8 teaspoon salt
- 1 tablespoon mayonnaise
- 1/8 teaspoon of cayenne pepper
- 1/8 teaspoon of curry powder
- 6 eggs, shelled
- 2 eggs, beaten lightly
- 1 oz. pork sausage
- 1/3 cup flour
- 1 cup bread crumbs

Instructions:

1. Combine the chutney, yogurt, pepper, salt, mayonnaise, cayenne, and curry powder in a bowl. Refrigerate.
2. Divide your pork sausage into 6 portions evenly and fatten each portion into patties.
3. Place an egg at the center. Wrap your sausage around the egg, sealing all sides.
4. Preheat your fryer to 390 F. Keep the beaten eggs in a bowl and flour in another bowl.
5. Place the bread crumbs on a plate.
6. Dip the sausage-wrapped eggs in the flour and then into your beaten eggs, shaking the excess.
7. Roll in the bread crumbs and place on a plate.
8. Apply cooking spray and keep it in the basket. Cook for 12 minutes, turning the eggs halfway.
9. Serve with the dipping sauce.

Nutrition Facts Per Serving

Calories 501, Carbohydrates 21g, Cholesterol 284mg, Total Fat 37g, Protein 21g, Sugar 3g, Fiber 0.4g, Sodium 945mg, Potassium 308mg

Cheese and Chicken Enchiladas

Prep Time: 15 minutes, Cook Time: 40 minutes, Serves: 6

Ingredients:

- ½ cup sour cream
- 1 can condensed cream of chicken soup
- 2 teaspoons of chili powder
- 1 cup Picante sauce
- ½ cup jack cheese
- 2 cups cooked chicken, chopped
- 1 tomato, chopped
- 6 flour tortillas
- 1 onion, sliced

Instructions:

1. Stir the sour cream, soup, chili powder, and Picante sauce in a bowl. Pour in a cup of the soup mix, cheese, and chicken.
2. Divide your chicken mix among the tortillas, roll them up and keep on a baking dish.
3. Pour the remaining portion of the soup mix over your filled tortillas.
4. Cook for 40 minutes and top with onion and tomato.

Nutrition Facts Per Serving

Calories 347, Carbohydrates 23g, Cholesterol 60mg, Total Fat 19g, Protein 21g, Fiber 3g, Sodium 1039mg

Turkish Chicken Kebab

Prep Time: 45 minutes, Cook Time: 15 minutes, Serves: 4

Ingredients:

- 1 oz. Chicken thighs, boneless and skinless
- ¼ cup Greek yogurt, plain
- 1 tablespoon tomato paste
- 1 tablespoon vegetable oil
- ½ teaspoon cinnamon, ground

Instructions:

1. Stir together the tomato paste, Greek yogurt, oil, cinnamon, salt, and pepper in a bowl, until well combined.
2. Cut the chicken into 4 pieces. Dredge into the mixture to coat well. Refrigerate.
3. Take out chicken from your marinade and keep in your air fryer basket in a single layer.
4. Set your fryer to 370 degrees F and cook for 8 minutes. Flip over and cook for another 4 minutes. Once done, serve.

Nutrition Facts Per Serving

Calories 375, Carbohydrates 4g, Cholesterol 112mg, Total Fat 31g, Protein 20g, Sugar 1g, Fiber 1g

Popcorn Chicken

Prep Time: 15 minutes, Cook Time: 10 minutes, Serves: 4

Ingredients:

- 1 oz. chicken breast halves, boneless and skinless
- ½ teaspoon paprika
- ¼ teaspoon mustard, ground
- ¼ teaspoon of garlic powder
- 3 tablespoons of cornstarch

Instructions:

1. Cut the chicken into small pieces and keep in a bowl.
2. Combine the paprika, garlic powder, mustard, salt, and pepper in another bowl. Reserve a teaspoon of your seasoning mixture and sprinkle the other portion on the chicken, tossing to coat evenly.
3. Combine the reserved seasoning and cornstarch in a plastic bag, shaking to combine well.
4. Keep your chicken pieces in the bag. Seal and shake for coating evenly.
5. Transfer to a mesh strainer, shaking the excess cornstarch.
6. Preheat your air fryer to 390 degrees F.
7. Apply some oil on the air fryer basket, and keep the chicken pieces inside.
8. Apply cooking spray and cook until cooked through.

Nutrition Facts Per Serving

Calories 156, Carbohydrates 6g, Cholesterol 65mg, Total Fat 4g, Protein 24g, Sugar 0g, Fiber 0.3g, Sodium 493mg

Blackened Chicken Breast

Prep Time: 10 minutes, Cook Time: 15 minutes, Serves: 2

Ingredients:

- 2 chicken breast halves, skinless and boneless
- 1 teaspoon thyme, ground
- 2 teaspoons of paprika
- 2 teaspoons vegetable oil
- ½ teaspoon onion powder

Instructions:

1. Combine the thyme, paprika, onion powder, and salt in your bowl. Transfer the spice mix to a flat plate.
2. Rub vegetable oil on the chicken breast to coat fully.
3. Roll the chicken pieces in the spice mixture. Press down, ensuring that all sides have the spice mix.
4. Preheat your air fryer to 360 degrees F.
5. Keep the chicken in the air fryer basket and cook for 8 minutes. Flip once and cook for another 7 minutes.
6. Transfer to a serving plate. Serve after 5 minutes.

Nutrition Facts Per Serving

Calories 427, Carbohydrates 3g, Cholesterol 198mg, Total Fat 11g, Protein 79g, Sugar 1g, Fiber 2g, Sodium 516mg

Chapter 7 – Beef, Lamb, and Pork

Pulled Pork

Prep Time: 5 minutes, Cook Time: 45 minutes, Serves: 4

Ingredients:

- 1-1/2 lbs. pork loin, boneless
- 1 onion, halved and sliced
- 2 teaspoons chili powder
- 2 tablespoons of light brown sugar
- 2 tablespoons cider vinegar
- 1 can roasted red pepper soup
- 4 toasted hamburger buns

Instructions:

1. Keep onion in your pot and add in the pork seasoned with pepper and salt.
2. Sprinkle chili powder and brown sugar on top. Stir the vinegar and soup in a bowl and pour over the pork.
3. Close the lid and cook for 40 minutes. Release pressure naturally once cooked.
4. Transfer pork to your cutting board and shred. Then cook sauce mix for 5 minutes and pour it to the cooker, stir well.
5. Serve your pork mix over the buns.

Nutrition Facts Per Serving

Calories 391, Carbohydrates 33g, Cholesterol 91mg, Total Fat 11g, Protein 40g, Fiber 3g, Sodium 597mg

Beef Stroganoff

Prep Time: 10 minutes, Cook Time: 10 minutes, Serves: 6

Ingredients:

- 1-1/4 lbs. beef sirloin steak, boneless and cut into thin strips
- 1 onion, diced
- ½ teaspoon garlic powder
- 1 teaspoon paprika
- 2 cups of beef broth
- 4 cups of egg noodles, uncooked
- 1 can condensed cream of mushroom soup
- 2 teaspoons of Worcestershire sauce
- 2 tablespoons parsley, chopped
- ¼ cup of sour cream

Instructions:

1. Season the beef with pepper and salt.
2. Layer the beef, onion, garlic powder, noodles, and paprika in your pot. Pour the Worcestershire and broth over noodles and spoon soup on top.
3. Close the lid and cook for 8 minutes and release pressure once done.
4. Stir in sour cream and set it aside uncovered.
5. Sprinkle parsley and serve.

Nutrition Facts Per Serving

Calories 325, Carbohydrates 26g, Cholesterol 67mg, Total Fat 13g, Protein 26g, Fiber 2g, Sodium 707mg

Pork-Chipotle Tacos

Prep Time: 5 minutes, Cook Time: 15 minutes, Serves: 5

Ingredients:

- 1-1/2 lbs. of pork loin
- 1 teaspoon oil
- 1 jar chipotle sauce
- ½ cup of water

Instructions:

1. Heat oil in your pot and cook the meat for 6 minutes, stirring frequently.
2. Add in the sauce and water, no stirring. Close the lid and cook for 8 minutes.
3. Release pressure once done and serve.

Nutrition Facts Per Serving

Calories 295, Carbohydrates 14g, Cholesterol 75mg, Total Fat 15g, Protein 26g, Sugar 5g, Fiber 3g, Sodium 460mg

Breaded Pork Chops

Prep Time: 5 minutes, Cook Time: 10 minutes, Serves: 4

Ingredients:

- 1 teaspoon of Cajun seasoning
- 4 pork chops, boneless and center-cut
- 2 eggs
- 1-1/2 cups of garlic and cheese flavored croutons

Instructions:

1. Preheat your air fryer to 390 degrees F.
2. Keep the pork chops on a plate and season both sides with Cajun seasoning.
3. Pulse croutons in your food processor, then transfer to a dish.
4. Beat the eggs lightly in another dish; and dip your pork chops into it, shaking off the excess.
5. Coat chops in the crouton breading and keep on a plate.
6. Apply cooking spray on chops, and cook for 5 minutes in your air fryer, flipping halfway.
7. Apply some more cooking spray and cook for another 5 minutes. Serve.

Nutrition Facts Per Serving

Calories 436, Carbohydrates 10g, Cholesterol 218mg, Total Fat 24g, Protein 45g, Sugar 1g, Fiber 1g, Sodium 429mg, Potassium 758mg

Air Fryer Pork Meatballs

Prep Time: 10 minutes, Cook Time: 20 minutes, Serves: 12

Ingredients:

- 12 oz. pork, ground
- 8 oz. Italian sausage, ground
- 1 egg
- ½ cup panko bread crumbs
- 1 teaspoon parsley, dried
- 1 teaspoon salt
- ½ teaspoon paprika

Instructions:

1. Preheat your fryer to 350 degrees F.
2. Bring together the sausage, pork, egg, bread crumbs, paprika, and parsley in a bowl, combine well.
3. Create 12 same-sized meatballs with your ice cream scoop and keep them on your baking sheet.
4. Place 6 meatballs in your air fryer basket and cook for 7 minutes, shaking halfway. Cook for another 3 minutes.
5. Take out and transfer on a serving plate. Repeat the process with the other meatballs.

Nutrition Facts Per Serving

Calories 147, Carbohydrates 4g, Cholesterol 41mg, Total Fat 11g, Protein 8g, Sugar 0g, Fiber 0g, Sodium 391mg, Potassium 119mg

Rosemary Garlic Lamb Chops

Prep Time: 3 minutes, Cook Time: 10 minutes, Serves: 2

Ingredients:

- 4 chops of lamb
- 1 teaspoon olive oil
- 2 teaspoon garlic puree
- Fresh garlic
- Fresh rosemary

Instructions:

1. Keep your lamb chops in the fryer grill pan.
2. Season the chops with pepper and salt and brush some olive oil on it.
3. Add some garlic puree on each chop. Cover the grill pan gaps with garlic cloves and rosemary sprigs.
4. Refrigerate the grill pan to marinate. Keep in the fryer and cook for 5 minutes, turning over.
5. Add some olive oil to cook for another 5 minutes. Set aside for a minute.
6. Take out the rosemary and garlic before serving.

Nutrition Facts Per Serving

Calories 678, Carbohydrates 1g, Cholesterol 257mg, Total Fat 38g, Protein 83g, Sugar 0g, Sodium 200mg

Braised Lamb Shanks

Prep Time: 15 minutes, Cook Time: 2 hours, 30 minutes, Serves: 4

Ingredients:

- 4 lamb shanks
- 4 crushed garlic cloves
- 2 tablespoons of olive oil
- 3 cups of beef broth
- 2 tablespoons balsamic vinegar

Instructions:

1. Season your lamb shanks with pepper and salt, keep in the baking pan.
2. Rub the smashed garlic and olive oil on the lamb well.
3. Cut the shanks and keep underneath your lamb.
4. Place the pan into the rack. Roast for 20 minutes at 425 degrees F, then cook at 250 degrees F on Low, about 2 hours.
5. Add vinegar and 2 cups of broth, stir in the remaining broth after the 1st hour.
6. Once done, serve.

Nutrition Facts Per Serving

Calories 453, Carbohydrates 6g, Cholesterol 121mg, Total Fat 37g, Protein 24g, Fiber 2g, Sodium 578mg

Italian-Style Meatballs

Prep Time: 10 minutes, Cook Time: 25 minutes, Serves: 12

Ingredients:

- 10 oz. lean beef, ground
- 3 garlic cloves, minced
- 5 oz. turkey sausage
- 2 tablespoons shallot, minced
- 1 large egg, lightly beaten
- 2 tablespoons of olive oil
- 1 tablespoon of rosemary and thyme, chopped

Instructions:

1. Preheat your air fryer to 400 degrees F.
2. Heat oil and add the shallot and cook for 1-2 minutes.
3. Cook the garlic, then take out from the heat.
4. Add the garlic and cooked shallot along with the egg, turkey sausage, beef, rosemary, thyme, and salt to combine well by stirring.
5. Shape the mixture gently into 1-1/2 inch small balls and keep in your air fryer basket.
6. Cook at 400 degrees F for 20 minutes. Once done, take out.
7. Keep warm and serve over rice or pasta.

Nutrition Facts Per Serving

Calories 175, Carbohydrates 0g, Total Fat 15g, Fiber 0g, Protein 10g, Sugar 0g, Sodium 254mg

Air Fryer BBQ Ribs

Prep Time: 5 minutes, Cook Time: 35 minutes, Serves: 4

Ingredients:

- 1 tablespoon of brown sugar
- 3 oz. baby back pork ribs
- 1 teaspoon of sweet paprika
- 1 teaspoon of smoked paprika
- 1 tablespoon white sugar
- 1 teaspoon granulated garlic
- ½ teaspoon granulated onion
- ½ teaspoon cumin, ground
- ½ teaspoon black pepper, ground
- ¼ teaspoon of Greek seasoning
- 1/3 cup BBQ sauce

Instructions:

1. Preheat your air fryer to 350 degrees F.
2. Strip off the membrane from the rib's back and cut into 4 same-sized portions.
3. Add together the sugars, paprika, pepper, garlic, onion, cumin, and the Greek seasoning in a bowl. Then rub the spice mix over the ribs.
4. Keep in your fryer basket and cook for 30 minutes, turning halfway through.
5. Brush BBQ sauce and fry for another 5 minutes. Serve.

Nutrition Facts Per Serving

Calories 744, Carbohydrates 15g, Total Fat 60g, Cholesterol 176mg, Fiber 1g, Protein 36g, Sugar 12g, Sodium 415mg, Potassium 565mg

Steak and Mushrooms

Prep Time: 5 minutes, Cook Time: 10 minutes, Serves: 4

Ingredients:

- ½ oz. sliced button mushrooms
- 1 oz. beef sirloin steak, cubed
- 1 tablespoon of olive oil
- ¼ cup Worcestershire sauce
- 1 teaspoon of paprika
- 1 teaspoon parsley flakes
- 1 teaspoon chili flakes, crushed

Instructions:

1. Combine the mushrooms, steak, olive oil, Worcestershire sauce, chili flakes, paprika, and parsley in a bowl. Refrigerate overnight.
2. Preheat your fryer at 400 degrees F.
3. Drain and remove the marinade from your steak mix.
4. Keep the mushrooms and steak in your air fryer basket, cook for 5 minutes.
5. Toss and cook for another 5 minutes then transfer to a serving plate.

Nutrition Facts Per Serving

Calories 261, Carbohydrates 6g, Total Fat 17g, Cholesterol 60mg, Fiber 1g, Protein 21g, Sugar 3g, Sodium 213mg, Potassium 590mg

Pork Tenderloin with Green Beans & Potatoes

Prep Time: 10 minutes, Cook Time: 30 minutes, Serves: 4

Ingredients:

- 2 tablespoons of brown sugar
- ¼ cup Dijon mustard
- ½ teaspoon thyme, dried
- 1 teaspoon parsley flakes, dried
- ¼ teaspoon black pepper, ground
- ¼ teaspoon salt
- ½ oz. potatoes, halved
- 1-1/4 oz. pork tenderloins
- 1 tablespoon of olive oil
- 1 pack green beans, trimmed

Instructions:

1. Preheat your air fryer to 400 degrees F.
2. Whisk together the brown sugar, mustard, thyme, parsley, pepper, and salt in a bowl. Pour the mixture over the tenderloin.
3. Roll through your mustard mix to coat all sides evenly.
4. Place the beans, potatoes, and olive oil in another bowl.
5. Season the the tenderloin with pepper and salt. Set aside.
6. Keep in the fryer basket and cook for 20 minutes. Take out and place on your cutting board.
7. Place potatoes and beans in the basket and cook for 10 minutes, shaking the basket halfway through.
8. Slice and serve with the beans and potatoes.

Nutrition Facts Per Serving

Calories 296, Carbohydrates 31g, Total Fat 8g, Cholesterol 61mg, Fiber 4g, Protein 25g, Sugar 8g, Sodium 620mg, Potassium 548mg

Roast Beef

Prep Time: 5 minutes, Cook Time: 40 minutes, Serves: 6

Ingredients:

- 2 oz. beef roast
- 1 tablespoon olive oil
- 2 teaspoon thyme and rosemary
- 1 teaspoon of salt
- 1 onion, medium

Instructions:

1. Preheat your air fryer to 390 degrees F.
2. Mix the rosemary, oil, and salt on a plate.
3. Use paper towels to pat dry your beef roast and coat the oil-herb mix on the outside. Keep coated beef roast in the air fryer basket.
4. Peel the onion and cut it in half. Then keep the halves next to your roast.
5. Cook for 12 minutes. Reduce the heat and cook for another 25 minutes at 360 degrees F.
6. Take it out and cover using kitchen foil. Carve it thinly against the grain.
7. Serve with steamed or roasted vegetables, gravy, and wholegrain mustard.

Nutrition Facts Per Serving

Calories 221, Carbohydrates 2g, Cholesterol 83mg, Total Fat 9g, Protein 33g, Fiber 1g, Sugar 1g, Sodium 282mg

Rice, Sweet Potato & Lamb

Prep Time: 5 minutes, Cook Time: 10 minutes, Serves: 2

Ingredients:

- ¼ cup lamb, cooked and puréed
- ½ cup cooked brown rice
- ¼ cup of sweet potato purée

Instructions:

1. Keep all the ingredients in your bowl, pulse until well combined.
2. Process with milk to get a smoother consistency.
3. Store in an airtight container. Refrigerate.

Nutrition Facts Per Serving

Calories 37, Carbohydrates 5g, Cholesterol 7mg, Total Fat 1g, Protein 2g, Fiber 1g, Sodium 6mg

Basic Hot Dogs

Prep Time: 5 minutes, Cook Time: 5 minutes, Serves: 4

Ingredients:

- 4 hot dogs
- 4 hot dog buns

Instructions:

1. Preheat your air fryer at 390 degrees F.
2. Keep the buns in your fryer basket and cook for 2 minutes. Then take out and keep on a plate.
3. Now place the hot dogs in the fryer basket and cook for 3 minutes.
4. Transfer them to the buns and serve.

Nutrition Facts Per Serving

Calories 317, Carbohydrates 23g, Cholesterol 24mg, Total Fat 21g, Protein 9g, Fiber 1g, Sugar 4g, Sodium 719mg, Potassium 111mg

Air Fryer Pizza Dogs

Prep Time: 5 minutes, Cook Time: 5 minutes, Serves: 2

Ingredients:

- 4 pepperoni slices, halved
- 2 hot dogs
- 2 hot dog buns
- ½ cup pizza sauce
- 2 teaspoons olives, sliced
- ¼ cup mozzarella cheese, shredded

Instructions:

1. Preheat your air fryer to 390 degrees F.
2. Create four slits in each hot dog. Keep them in your fryer basket and cook for 3 minutes.
3. Use tongs to transfer them to your cutting board and place a pepperoni half in every hot dog slit.
4. Now divide the pizza sauce between the buns. Fill with the olives, mozzarella cheese, and hot dogs.
5. Keep the hot dogs in the fryer basket again and cook for 2 minutes. Once done, serve.

Nutrition Facts Per Serving

Calories 535, Carbohydrates 28g, Cholesterol 57mg, Total Fat 39g, Protein 18g, Fiber 2g, Sugar 6g, Sodium 1408mg, Potassium 172mg

Lamb Sirloin Steak

Prep Time: 5 minutes, Cook Time: 10 minutes, Serves: 4

Ingredients:

- 1 oz. lamb sirloin steaks, boneless
- 5 garlic cloves
- 1 teaspoon fennel, ground
- ½ onion
- 1 teaspoon cinnamon, ground

Instructions:

1. Add all the ingredients in your blender bowl other than the lamb chops.
2. Pulse and blend to well combined or until the onion is minced fine.
3. Now keep your lamb chops in a big-sized bowl and slash the meat and fat with a knife to coat well with marinade and spice paste. Mix well and refrigerate.
4. Keep the steaks of lamb in your air fryer basket and cook, flipping once.

Nutrition Facts Per Serving

Calories 189, Carbohydrates 3g, Total Fat 9g, Protein 24g, Fiber 1g

Chapter 8 – Vegan and Vegetarian

Vegetable & Coconut Curry Rice Bowl

Prep Time: 15 minutes, Cook Time: 20 minutes, Serves: 6

Ingredients:

- 1 teaspoon curry powder
- 2/3 cup brown rice, rinsed and drained
- 1 cup of water
- 1 cup onion, chopped
- ¾ teaspoon salt
- 1 cup carrots
- 1 cup yellow or red bell pepper, sliced
- 1 can water chestnuts, sliced and drained
- 1 cup purple or red cabbage, chopped
- 13 oz. coconut milk
- 15 oz. chickpeas, rinsed and drained
- 1-1/2 tablespoons of sugar
- 1 tablespoon ginger, grated

Instructions:

1. Combine the curry powder, water, rice, and ¼ teaspoon of salt in your pot.
2. Close the lid and cook for 15 minutes. Release pressure naturally.
3. Open the lid and stir the other ingredients in.
4. Now boil for 5 minutes. Stir occasionally.

Nutrition Facts Per Serving

Calories 258, Carbohydrates 42g, Cholesterol 0mg, Total Fat 10g, Protein 8g, Fiber 7g, Sugar 9g, Sodium 330mg, Potassium 540mg

Ginger, Edamame Spaghetti and Lime Squash

Prep Time: 20 minutes, Cook Time: 15 minutes, Serves: 6

Ingredients:

- 3 tablespoons of soy sauce, low-sodium
- 1 spaghetti squash
- 1 cup of water
- 4 teaspoons sugar
- 2 limes
- 1/8 teaspoon pepper flakes, crushed
- 1 tablespoon ginger, grated
- 1 cup carrots
- 12 oz. edamame, shelled
- 2 oz. peanuts or almonds, unsalted and chopped
- ½ cup onion
- ½ cup cilantro, chopped

Instructions:

1. Use a knife to pierce your squash. Keep in the microwave for 2 minutes; take it out and cut crosswise. Remove the connecting strands and seeds.
2. Pour water into your pot and the squash halves on your trivet. Close the lid and cook for 7 minutes. Release pressure.
3. Combine the juice of one lime, ginger, soy sauce, sugar, and the pepper flakes in a bowl. Whisk well. Set aside.
4. Take out your squash halves and keep on the cutting board.
5. Now include edamame to the water and boil for 3 minutes. Drain.
6. Run your fork around the squash's outer edges to make long spaghetti strands.
7. Keep the squash in a serving bowl. Top with carrots, onion, and edamame.
8. Now spoon the soy sauce mix on top and sprinkle cilantro and nuts.
9. Cut the remaining lime portion into six wedges. Serve with your squash.

Nutrition Facts Per Serving

Calories 205, Carbohydrates 21g, Cholesterol 0mg, Total Fat 9g, Protein 10g, Fiber 6g, Sugar 9g, Sodium 320mg, Potassium 820mg

Spinach Lasagna Rolls

Prep Time: 15 minutes, Cook Time: 12 minutes, Serves: 4

Ingredients:

- 15 oz. ricotta cheese
- ½ cup Parmesan cheese
- 1 cup of water
- 4 cloves of garlic, minced
- 1 cup spinach, chopped
- ¼ teaspoon of black pepper
- ½ teaspoon salt
- 8 cooked lasagna noodles
- 1-1/4 cups of pasta sauce

Instructions:

1. Pour water into your pot.
2. Combine the ricotta, ¼ cup Parmesan, spinach, garlic, pepper, and salt in a bowl. Mix well.
3. Spread ¼ cup pasta sauce at the bottom of your pan.
4. Now lay the cooked lasagna noodles flat and spread the ricotta filling on top of your noodles.
5. Roll the lasagna noodle lengthwise then spread the remaining sauce portion over the rolls.
6. Keep Parmesan cheese on top.
7. Close the lid of your pot and cook for 12 minutes. Release pressure and open.

Nutrition Facts Per Serving

Calories 483, Carbohydrates 51g, Total Fat 19g, Protein 27g, Fiber 4g, Sugar 4g, Sodium 936mg

Vegetable Tian

Prep Time: 10 minutes, Cook Time: 35 minutes, Serves: 4

Ingredients:

- ½ onion, peeled and diced
- 1 tablespoon olive oil
- 1 cup of water
- 2 cloves of garlic, minced
- 1 zucchini, cut into half-inch slices
- 1 yellow squash, cut into half-inch slices
- 1 russet potato, cut into half-inch slices
- 2 Roma tomatoes, cut into half-inch slices
- 1/8 teaspoon black pepper
- ¼ teaspoon salt
- ¼ cup Parmesan cheese, grated
- ½ cup mozzarella cheese, shredded

Instructions:

1. Add garlic, onion and oil to your pot and cook for 5 minutes.
2. Take out the onion and garlic. Keep in a pan.
3. Clean the inside of your pot and keep them back in it. Add trivet and water to your pot.
4. Arrange the zucchini, squash, potato, and tomato around the edge of the pan.
5. Cover the pan's top with a paper towel and foil. Lower it into the pot; close the lid and cook for 30 minutes.
6. Release the pressure once done and unlock the lid.
7. Take out. Sprinkle mozzarella, Parmesan cheese, pepper, and salt.

Nutrition Facts Per Serving

Calories 200, Carbohydrates 23g, Total Fat 8g, Protein 9g, Fiber 3g, Sugar 4g, Sodium 260mg

Roasted Cauliflower and Broccoli

Prep Time: 5 minutes, Cook Time: 15 minutes, Serves: 6

Ingredients:

- 3 cups cauliflower florets
- 3 cups of broccoli florets
- ¼ teaspoon of sea salt
- ½ teaspoon of garlic powder
- 2 tablespoons olive oil

Instructions:

1. Preheat your air fryer to 400 degrees F.
2. Keep your florets of broccoli in a microwave-safe bowl. Cook in your microwave for 3 minutes at high temperature.
3. Now add the olive oil, cauliflower, sea salt, and garlic powder to the broccoli in the bowl. Combine well by mixing.
4. Pour this mix now into your air fryer basket. Cook for 10 minutes and toss the vegetables after 5 minutes.

Nutrition Facts Per Serving

Calories 77, Carbohydrates 6g, Cholesterol 0mg, Total Fat 5g, Protein 2g, Sugar 2g, Fiber 3g, Sodium 103mg

Stuffed Pumpkin

Prep Time: 5 minutes, Cook Time: 25 minutes, Serves: 2

Ingredients:

- ½ pumpkin, small
- 1 sweet potato, diced
- 1 parsnip, diced
- 1 carrot, diced

Instructions:

1. Scrape out the seeds from the pumpkin.
2. Combine the sweet potato, parsnip, carrot, and the egg in a bowl.
3. Fill up your pumpkin with this vegetable mixture.
4. Preheat your air fryer to 350 degrees F.
5. Keep your stuffed pumpkin in the fryer's basket. Cook for 25 minutes until tender.

Nutrition Facts Per Serving

Calories 268, Carbohydrates 49g, Cholesterol 93mg, Total Fat 4g, Protein 9g, Sugar 13g, Fiber 10g, Sodium 210mg

Air Fryer Plantain

Prep Time: 5 minutes, Cook Time: 15 minutes, Serves: 4

Ingredients:

- 2 plantains, unripe
- 3 cups of water
- Olive oil cooking spray
- Salt to taste

Instructions:

1. Preheat your fryer to 400 degrees F.
2. Slice the plantain tips. Cut the thick skin but don't cut the flesh.
3. Now cut the plantain into one-inch chunks, with the peel on.
4. Peel off the skin from the chunks. Keep the chunks in your fryer basket.
5. Apply the olive oil spray and fry for 5 minutes.
6. Prepare a salted water bowl meanwhile.
7. Take out the pieces from your fryer. Smash them to half-inch thickness and soak them in your salted water bowl. Remove them from the bowl and pat dry with a paper towel.
8. Bring back the plantain to your fryer.
9. Apply olive oil on top and season with salt. Cook for 5 minutes. Apply more olive oil spray. Flip and cook for another 5 minutes.

Nutrition Facts Per Serving

Calories 125, Carbohydrates 28g, Cholesterol 0mg, Total Fat 1g, Protein 1g, Sugar 13g, Fiber 2g, Sodium 48mg, Potassium 448mg

Vegan Fried Ravioli

Prep Time: 10 minutes, Cook Time: 10 minutes, Serves: 4

Ingredients:

- 2 teaspoons of nutritional yeast flakes
- ½ cup bread crumbs
- 1 teaspoon oregano, dried
- 1 teaspoon basil, dried
- ¼ cup of aquafaba liquid from a can of chickpeas
- 1 teaspoon of garlic powder
- 11/ oz. vegan ravioli
- ½ cup marinara
- Pinch of pepper and salt

Instructions:

1. Combine the nutritional yeast flakes, bread crumbs, garlic powder, basil, oregano, pepper, and salt on a plate.
2. Keep the aquafaba in a bowl. Now dip your ravioli into the aquafaba. Remove the excess liquid.
3. Dredge in the bread crumb mix.
4. Keep the ravioli in your fryer basket.
5. Apply cooking spray and cook for 6 minutes. Flip and cook for another 4 minutes.
6. Take them out and serve with the marinara for dipping.

Nutrition Facts Per Serving

Calories 128, Carbohydrates 27g, Protein 5g, Sugar 1g, Fiber 2g, Sodium 411mg, Potassium 145mg

Roasted Vegetables

Prep Time: 10 minutes, Cook Time: 15 minutes, Serves: 4

Ingredients:

- 1 yellow squash, cut into small pieces
- 1 red bell pepper, seeded and cut into small pieces
- ¼ oz. mushrooms, cleaned and halved
- 1 tablespoon of extra-virgin olive oil
- 1 zucchini, cut into small pieces

Instructions:

1. Preheat your air fryer. Keep the squash, red bell pepper, and mushrooms in a bowl.
2. Add the black pepper, salt, and olive oil. Combine well by tossing.
3. Air fry the vegetables in your fryer basket for 15 minutes until roasted. Stir halfway.

Nutrition Facts Per Serving

Calories 89, Carbohydrates 8g, Cholesterol 0mg, Total Fat 5g, Protein 3g, Sugar 4g, Fiber 2.3g, Sodium 48mg

Fried Chickpeas

Prep Time: 5 minutes, Cook Time: 20 minutes, Serves: 4

Ingredients:

- 1 can chickpeas, rinsed and drained
- 1 tablespoon olive oil
- 1 tablespoon of nutritional yeast
- 1 teaspoon garlic, granulated
- 1 teaspoon of smoked paprika

Instructions:

1. Spread the chickpeas on paper towels. Cover using a second paper towel later to dry for half an hour.
2. Preheat your air fryer to 355 degrees F.
3. Bring together the nutritional yeast, chickpeas, smoked paprika, olive oil, salt, and garlic in a mid-sized bowl. Coat well by tossing.
4. Now add your chickpeas to the fryer. Cook for 16 minutes until crispy. Shake them in 4-minute intervals.

Nutrition Facts Per Serving

Calories 133, Carbohydrates 17g, Cholesterol 0mg, Total Fat 5g, Protein 5g, Sugar 0g, Fiber 4g, Sodium 501mg

Air Fryer Lemon Tofu

Prep Time: 10 minutes, Cook Time: 10 minutes, Serves: 4

Ingredients:

- 1 tablespoon tamari
- 1 oz. tofu, drained and pressed, extra-firm
- 1-1/2 tablespoons of arrowroot powder or cornstarch
- 1/3 cup of lemon juice
- 1 teaspoon of lemon zest
- 2 tablespoons organic sugar
- ½ cup of water

Instructions:

1. Cube the tofu. Keep in a plastic storage bag.
2. Include the tamari. Seal the bag and shake until the tofu is well coated with the tamari.
3. Now add the tablespoon cornstarch to this bag. Shake well. Tofu should be nicely coated. Set aside to marinate.
4. Add all your sauce ingredients meanwhile to a bowl. Mix well and set aside.
5. Keep your tofu in the fryer and cook for 10 minutes. Add them to a skillet over high heat.
6. Stir the sauce and pour this over your tofu. Now stir until the sauce thickens.
7. Serve with the steamed vegetables and rice.

Nutrition Facts Per Serving

Calories 111, Carbohydrates 13g, Total Fat 3g, Protein 8g, Sugar 8g, Sodium 294mg, Potassium 250mg

Vegan Beignets

Prep Time: 15 minutes, Cook Time: 20 minutes, Serves: 24

Ingredients:

- 1 teaspoon corn starch
- 1 cup sweetener baking blend
- 3 tablespoons of baking blend
- 1 cup coconut milk, full-fat
- 1-1/2 teaspoons of baking yeast
- 3 tablespoons of aquafaba
- 2 tablespoons of coconut oil, melted
- 3 cups white flour
- 2 teaspoons of vanilla

Instructions:

1. Add the corn starch and baking blend to your blender. Blend.
2. Heat your coconut milk, then add to the mixture with the yeast and sugar. Set aside.
3. Now mix in the aquafaba, coconut oil, vanilla and flour.
4. Knead the dough and keep in your mixing bowl.
5. Sprinkle a bit of flour on your cutting board.
6. Make a rectangle from the dough. Create 24 squares.
7. Preheat your fryer to 390 degrees F and cook one side for 3 minutes. Flip and cook for 2 more minutes.
8. Sprinkle your powdered baking blend liberally. Preheat the oven to 350 degrees F.
9. Keep the beignets on a baking sheet covering parchment paper.
10. Bake for 15 minutes. Sprinkle the baking blend liberally.

Nutrition Facts Per Serving

Calories 126, Carbohydrates 15g, Cholesterol 0mg, Total Fat 6g, Protein 3g, Sugar 1g, Fiber 1g, Sodium 2mg

Seitan Riblets

Prep Time: 10 minutes, Cook Time: 20 minutes, Serves: 4

Ingredients:

- ¼ cup of nutritional yeast
- 1 cup of wheat gluten
- 1 teaspoon of onion powder
- 1 teaspoon mushroom powder
- ½ teaspoon garlic powder
- 1 teaspoon salt
- ¼ cup barbecue sauce
- ¾ cup of water

Instructions:

1. Add the wheat gluten, mushroom powder, nutritional yeast, garlic powder, salt, and onion powder to the food processor. Mix well.
2. Drizzle water and run the processor for 4 minutes.
3. Take out the dough and knead on your cutting board. Create a square or circle to fit the air fryer basket.
4. Place the seitan pieces in the fryer and cook for 8 minutes at 370 degrees F. Flip and cook for 6 more minutes.
5. Cut into chunks or slice for sandwiches.

Nutrition Facts Per Serving

Calories 291, Carbohydrates 19g, Cholesterol 0mg, Total Fat 3g, Protein 47g, Sugar 6g, Fiber 3g, Sodium 787mg

Chapter 9 – Desserts

Fruit Crumble

Prep Time: 10 minutes, Cook Time: 15 minutes, Serves: 2

Ingredients:

- ½ cup strawberries or blueberries
- 1 apple, diced
- 2 tablespoons of sugar
- ½ cup tablespoon of brown rice flour
- 2 tablespoons butter
- ½ teaspoon cinnamon, ground

Instructions:

1. Preheat your air fryer to 350 degrees F.
2. Bring together the berries and apples in a baking pan.
3. Combine the sugar, flour, butter, and cinnamon in a bowl.
4. Now spoon your flour mix over the fruit.
5. Sprinkle some more flour, covering exposed fruit. Cook for 15 minutes.

Nutrition Facts Per Serving

Calories 379, Carbohydrates 50g, Cholesterol 31mg, Total Fat 19g, Protein 2g, Sugar 26g, Fiber 5g, Sodium 5mg

Pumpkin Pudding with Vanilla-Apple Sauce

Prep Time: 15 minutes, Cook Time: 45 minutes, Serves: 8

Ingredients:

- 2 eggs
- 1-1/2 cups of milk
- 1/3 cup sugar
- ¾ cup of canned pumpkin
- 1 tablespoon of pumpkin pie spice
- 1 tablespoon butter with canola oil
- 1/8 teaspoon salt
- 2 teaspoons vanilla extract
- 1-1/4 cups of water
- 8 oz. Italian loaf bread, multigrain
- 1-1/2 teaspoon cornstarch
- ¾ cup of apple juice

Instructions:

1. Apply cooking spray on a pan.
2. Whisk together the pumpkin, eggs, milk, butter, sugar, vanilla extract, salt, and the pumpkin pie spice in a bowl. Blend well.
3. Include the bread cubes. Coat well by tossing. Set aside.
4. Keep your bread mix in the pan. Cover the pan with a foil.
5. Keep a trivet and water in your pot. Close the lid and cook for 40 minutes.
6. Release pressure and take out the lid.
7. Take out the pan and remove the trivet. Discard the water.
8. Mix the cornstarch and apple juice in a bowl.
9. Add the juice mix and the remaining portion of sugar to your pot. Boil for a minute.
10. Stir in the vanilla extract and the remaining butter.
11. Cut your pudding into wedges. Serve with the sauce.

Nutrition Facts Per Serving

Calories 662, Carbohydrates 28g, Cholesterol 55mg, Total Fat 58g, Protein 7g, Sugar 15g, Fiber 3g, Sodium 230mg, Potassium 230mg

Greek Yogurt Cheesecake

Prep Time: 10 minutes, Cook Time: 35 minutes, Serves: 8

Ingredients:

- 1-1/2 tablespoons butter, melted
- 6 cracker sheets
- ¾ cup plain Greek yogurt
- 8 oz. cream cheese
- 1 teaspoon vanilla extract
- 1/3 cup honey or agave nectar
- 1 cup sliced strawberries or raspberries
- 3 eggs
- 1 cup of water

Instructions:

1. Use parchment paper to line the base of your pan.
2. Apply butter on the parchment paper and both sides of your pan.
3. Process the crackers in your food processor.
4. Transfer your crumb mix to the pan. Press firmly to the bottom. Wipe off any crumbs from your food processor.
5. Combine the yogurt, cream cheese, vanilla, eggs, and nectar/agave in your food processor.
6. Pour filling into your crust. Remove the air bubbles.
7. Use aluminum foil to cover your pan.
8. Pour water into the pot. Close the lid and cook for 35 minutes.
9. Release pressure naturally once done. Take out and remove excess moisture from the top of your cheesecake. Set aside to cool.
10. Cut your cake into wedges. Serve with berries.

Nutrition Facts Per Serving

Calories 247, Carbohydrates 21g, Total Fat 15g, Protein 7g, Fiber 0g

Apple Fritters

Prep Time: 10 minutes, Cook Time: 10 minutes, Serves: 4

Ingredients:

- 1 apple – cored, peeled, and chopped
- 1 cup all-purpose flour
- 1 egg
- ½ cup milk
- 1-1/2 teaspoons of baking powder
- 2 tablespoons white sugar

Instructions:

1. Preheat your air fryer to 350 degrees F.
2. Keep parchment paper at the bottom of your fryer. Apply cooking spray, and mix ¼ cup sugar, flour, baking powder, egg, milk, and salt in a bowl. Combine well by stirring.
3. Sprinkle 2 tablespoons of sugar on the apples. Coat well.
4. Combine the apples into your flour mixture. Use a cookie scoop and drop the fritters with it to the air fryer basket's bottom.
5. Now air fry for 5 minutes. Flip and fry for another 3 minutes until golden.

Nutrition Facts Per Serving

Calories 307, Carbohydrates 65g, Cholesterol 48mg, Total Fat 3g, Protein 5g, Sugar 39g, Fiber 2g, Sodium 248mg

Roasted Bananas

Prep Time: 2 minutes, Cook Time: 7 minutes, Serves: 1

Ingredients:

- 1 banana, sliced into diagonal pieces
- Avocado oil cooking spray

Instructions:

1. Take parchment paper and line the air fryer basket with it.
2. Preheat your air fryer to 375 degrees F.
3. Keep your slices of banana in the basket.
4. Apply avocado oil and cook for 5 minutes.
5. Take out the basket. Flip the slices carefully.
6. Cook for 2 more minutes. The slices of banana should be caramelized and brown. Take them out from the basket.

Nutrition Facts Per Serving

Calories 121, Carbohydrates 27g, Cholesterol 0mg, Total Fat 1g, Protein 1g, Sugar 14g, Fiber 3g, Sodium 1mg

Chocolate Cherry Cake

Prep Time: 20 minutes, Cook Time: 30 minutes, Serves: 6

Ingredients:

- ¾ cup of vegetable oil
- 1 cup of water
- 2 eggs
- ¾ cup of granulated sugar
- 1-1/4 cups cake flour
- 2 teaspoons vanilla extract
- ½ teaspoon salt
- 6 tablespoons of cocoa powder, unsweetened
- 1 teaspoon baking soda
- ½ cup buttermilk
- 10 oz. maraschino cherries, chopped and juice reserved
- 1 teaspoon white vinegar
- ¼ cup butter, unsalted
- 1 cup of powdered sugar
- 1/8 cup of whole milk

Instructions:

1. Add the trivet and pour water into your pot.
2. Grease the pan and keep it aside. Cream the sugar and oil together.
3. Then add a teaspoon of vanilla and the eggs, 3 tablespoons of cocoa powder, flour, salt, the vinegar and baking soda in a bowl.
4. Add buttermilk and flour slowly to your mixer. Stir and pour into your cake batter, and mix for 10 seconds.
5. Fold in ½ of the chopped maraschino cherries.
6. Pour the cake batter into your pan and lower it into the pot. Close the lid and cook for 30 minutes.
7. Release pressure once done and take it out.
8. Create holes in your cake with a straw and pour cherry juice into them. Set the cake aside for cooling.
9. Now mix the remaining cocoa powder, butter, sugar, the remaining vanilla, and milk with an electric mixer.
10. Remove cake from the pan once cooled. Cut the edges with a butter knife.
11. Keep chocolate frosting on top and serve with the remaining cherries.

Nutrition Facts Per Serving

Calories 734, Carbohydrates 92g, Total Fat 38g, Protein 6g, Sugar 64g, Fiber 4g, Sodium 305mg

Air-Fried Butter Cake

Prep Time: 10 minutes, Cook Time: 15 minutes, Serves: 4

Ingredients:

- 7 tablespoons of butter
- 1/3 cup white sugar
- 1-2/3 cups of all-purpose flour
- 6 tablespoons of milk
- 1 egg
- Salt to taste

Instructions:

1. Preheat your air fryer to 350 degree F.
2. Using an electric butter, beat the butter in a bowl until creamy and light.
3. Add the egg, salt, flour and milk. Mix well.
4. Now transfer the batter to your pan. Level the surface with a spoon.
5. Keep the pan in your fryer basket and cook for 15 minutes.
6. Turn the cake and let it cool.

Nutrition Facts Per Serving

Calories 636, Carbohydrates 60g, Cholesterol 102mg, Total Fat 36g, Protein 8g, Sugar 20g, Fiber 1g, Sodium 210mg, Potassium 113mg

Chocolate Chip Cookies

Prep Time: 10 minutes, Cook Time: 15 minutes, Serves: 4

Ingredients:

- 1-1/2 oz. coconut sugar
- 9 oz. flour
- 5 oz. butter
- 3 oz. brown sugar
- 3 tablespoons whole milk
- 4 tablespoons of honey
- 1 teaspoon of vanilla essence
- 1 tablespoon of cocoa powder
- 3-1/2 oz. chocolate chips

Instructions:

1. Preheat your air fryer to 360 degrees F.
2. Keep the sugars and butter in a mixing bowl. Mix fat into the sugar until fluffy and light.
3. Now add the honey, flour, cocoa powder, vanilla, and milk. Mix well.
4. Make your hands covered with flour. Roll the chocolate chips in and mix well to create small cookie balls.
5. Keep the balls on a baking sheet in your fryer. Cook for 15 minutes.

Nutrition Facts Per Serving

Calories 1033, Carbohydrates 111g, Cholesterol 85mg, Total Fat 61g, Protein 10g, Sugar 60g, Fiber 3g, Sodium 317mg, Potassium 145mg

Lemon Biscuits

Prep Time: 5 minutes, Cook Time: 5 minutes, Serves: 9

Ingredients:

- 3-1/2 oz. caster sugar
- 3-1/2 oz. butter
- 1 lemon rind and juice
- 8 oz. flour
- 1 teaspoon vanilla essence
- 1 egg

Instructions:

1. Preheat your air fryer to 360 degrees F.
2. Mix sugar and flour in a bowl. Add butter and mix well. The fat parts should be on the top.
3. Now include the egg with the lemon rind and juice. Kneed and combine to have a soft dough. Then cut into mid-sized biscuits.
4. Keep the biscuits on a baking sheet inside your air fryer. Cook for 5 minutes.
5. Transfer to a cooling tray. Sprinkle icing sugar. Serve.

Nutrition Facts Per Serving

Calories 258, Carbohydrates 30g, Cholesterol 42mg, Total Fat 14g, Protein 3g, Sugar 11g, Fiber 0g, Sodium 87mg, Potassium 48mg

Cinnamon & Sugar Doughnuts

Prep Time: 10 minutes, Cook Time: 10 minutes, Serves: 9

Ingredients:

- 2 egg yolks
- 1-1/2 teaspoons baking powder
- 2-1/4 cups of all-purpose flour
- 2 tablespoons of butter
- ½ cup of white sugar
- ½ cup sour cream

Instructions:

1. Press butter and ½ cup of white sugar together in a bowl. Then add the egg yolks. Stir.
2. Now sift baking powder, flour, and salt into another bowl.
3. Place a third of the flour mix and half sour cream into your egg-sugar mix. Combine well.
4. Mix the remaining sour cream and flour in. Refrigerate.
5. Now mix 1/3rd cup of sugar.
6. Roll your dough to half-inch thickness. Cut into 9 circles, and create a small circle at the center of each circle. The shape should be like a doughnut.
7. Preheat your air fryer to 350 degrees F.
8. Brush half of the melted butter on both sides of your doughnut.
9. Transfer half of the doughnuts into your air fryer basket. Cook for 8 minutes.

Nutrition Facts Per Serving

Calories 336, Carbohydrates 44g, Cholesterol 66mg, Total Fat 16g, Protein 4g, Sugar 19g, Fiber 1g, Sodium 390mg

Chapter 10 – Snacks

Cheese Sticks

Prep Time: 10 minutes, Cook Time: 7 minutes, Serves: 6

Ingredients:

- 2 eggs
- 1 cheese sticks
- ¼ cup parmesan cheese, grated
- ¼ cup whole-wheat flour
- 1 teaspoon garlic powder
- 1 teaspoon of Italian seasoning
- ¼ teaspoon rosemary, ground

Instructions:

1. Unwrap the cheese sticks. Keep aside.
2. Beat the eggs into a bowl. Mix the cheese, seasonings, and flour in another bowl.
3. Now roll the sticks in the egg and then into the batter. Coat well.
4. Keep them in your air fryer basket. Cook for 7 minutes at 370 degrees F.
5. Serve hot.

Nutrition Facts Per Serving

Calories 76, Carbohydrates 5g, Cholesterol 75mg, Total Fat 4g, Protein 5g, Sugar 1g, Fiber 1g, Sodium 99mg, Potassium 50mg

Apple Chips

Prep Time: 2 minutes, Cook Time: 10 minutes, Serves: 4

Ingredients:

- 1 teaspoon olive oil
- 6 red apples
- 1 pinch of cinnamon

Instructions:

1. Cut the apples into bite-sized chunks.
2. Keep them in the air fryer, and drizzle 1 teaspoon of olive oil. Cook for 10 minutes at 365 degrees F until crispy.
3. Toss your apples in cinnamon in a bowl. Serve.

Nutrition Facts Per Serving

Calories 662, Carbohydrates 150g, Cholesterol 0mg, Total Fat 6g, Protein 2g, Sugar 113g, Fiber 26g, Sodium 11mg, Potassium 1168mg

Corn Nuts

Prep Time: 10 minutes, Cook Time: 20 minutes, Serves: 8

Ingredients:

- 1 oz. white corn
- 1-1/2 teaspoons salt
- 3 tablespoons of vegetable oil

Instructions:

1. Cover the corn with water in a bowl. Keep aside.
2. Drain the corn. Spread it on a baking sheet and use paper towels to pat dry.
3. Preheat your air fryer to 400 degrees F.
4. Transfer the corn to a bowl then add salt and oil. Stir to coat evenly.
5. Keep the corn in your air fryer basket. Cook for 8 minutes.
6. Shake the basket and cook for 10 minutes more.
7. Transfer to a plate lined with a paper towel. Set aside to cool.

Nutrition Facts Per Serving

Calories 240, Carbohydrates 36g, Cholesterol 0mg, Total Fat 8g, Protein 6g, Sugar 1g, Fiber 7g, Sodium 438mg

Baked Potatoes

Prep Time: 5 minutes, Cook Time: 1 hour, Serves: 2

Ingredients:

- 1 tablespoon peanut oil
- 2 large potatoes, scrubbed
- ½ teaspoon of coarse sea salt

Instructions:

1. Preheat your air fryer to 400 degrees F.
2. Brush peanut oil on your potatoes and sprinkle some salt. Then keep them in the basket of your air fryer.
3. Cook the potatoes for an hour. Serve hot.

Nutrition Facts Per Serving

Calories 360, Carbohydrates 64g, Cholesterol 0mg, Total Fat 8g, Protein 8g, Sugar 3g, Fiber 8g, Sodium 462mg

Chicken Nuggets

Prep Time: 10 minutes, Cook Time: 8 minutes, Serves: 4

Ingredients:

- ½ teaspoon black pepper
- ½ teaspoon kosher salt
- 16 oz. chicken breasts, skinless and boneless, cut into small pieces
- 6 tablespoons of whole-wheat Italian seasoned breadcrumbs
- 2 teaspoons of olive oil
- 2 tablespoons Parmesan cheese, grated
- 2 tablespoons of panko

Instructions:

1. Preheat your air fryer to 400 degrees F.
2. Place the panko, Parmesan cheese, and breadcrumbs in a bowl. Keep the olive oil in another bowl.
3. Season the chicken with pepper and salt and keep in the olive oil bowl. Mix well.
4. Keep a few chicken chunks into your breadcrumb mix, and then in the basket.
5. Apply cooking spray. Cook for 8 minutes. Turn halfway.

Nutrition Facts Per Serving

Calories 177, Carbohydrates 8g, Cholesterol 57mg, Total Fat 5g, Protein 25g, Sugar 1g, Sodium 427mg

Baked Cauliflower and Sweet Potato Patties

Prep Time: 15 minutes, Cook Time: 20 minutes, Serves: 7

Ingredients:

- 2 cups of cauliflower florets
- 1 sweet potato, peeled
- 1 teaspoon garlic, minced
- 1 green onion, chopped
- 1 cup cilantro
- 2 tablespoons of ranch or dairy seasoning mix
- ¼ teaspoon cumin
- ½ teaspoon of chili powder
- ¼ cup flaxseed, ground
- 2 tablespoons of arrowroot starch
- ¼ teaspoon pepper and kosher salt
- ¼ cup of sunflower seeds
- Dipping sauce

Instructions:

1. Preheat your oven to 400 degrees F.
2. Line your baking sheet. Set aside.
3. Cut the potatoes into small pieces and keep in your food processor. Pulse.
4. Add onion, garlic, and cauliflower. Pulse again.
5. Now add the flaxseed, sunflower seeds, cilantro, and remaining seasoning.
6. Keep the batter in a bowl. Scoop out ¼ cup to create 1.5-inch-thick patties.
7. Cook the patties on a baking sheet for 20 minutes. Refrigerate.

Nutrition Facts Per Serving

Calories 84, Carbohydrates 9g, Cholesterol 0mg, Total Fat 4g, Protein 3g, Fiber 3g, Sugar 2g, Sodium 200mg

Fried Green Tomatoes

Prep Time: 10 minutes, Cook Time: 15 minutes, Serves: 6

Ingredients:

- 2 tomatoes, cut into small slices
- ½ cup buttermilk
- 2 eggs, beaten lightly
- 1 cup bread crumbs
- 1/3 cup of all-purpose flour
- 1 cup yellow cornmeal

Instructions:

1. Season the slices of tomato with pepper and salt.
2. Take 3 breeding dishes. Keep flour in the first, stir in eggs and buttermilk in the second, and mix cornmeal and bread crumbs in the third.
3. Dredge the slices of tomato in your flour, shaking off any excess.
4. Now dip the tomatoes in the egg mix, then in the bread crumb mix to coat both sides.
5. Preheat your air fryer to 400 degrees F.
6. Brush olive oil on the fryer basket. Keep the slices of tomato in your fryer basket.
7. Brush some olive oil on the tomato tops, cook for 10 minutes. Flip your tomatoes, brush olive oil and cook for another 5 minutes.
8. Take the tomatoes out. Keep in a rack lined with a paper towel. Serve.

Nutrition Facts Per Serving

Calories 246, Carbohydrates 40g, Cholesterol 63mg, Total Fat 6g, Protein 8g, Sugar 3g, Fiber 2g, Sodium 166mg

Air Fried Chicken Tenders

Prep Time: 10 minutes, Cook Time: 10 minutes, Serves: 4

Ingredients:

- 1 egg white
- 12 oz. chicken breasts
- 1-1/4 oz. panko bread crumbs
- 1/8 cup flour
- Pepper and salt to taste
- Olive spray

Instructions:

1. Trim off excess fat from your chicken breast. Cut into tenders. Season with pepper and salt.
2. Dip the tenders into flour and then into egg whites and bread crumbs.
3. Keep in the fryer basket. Apply olive spray and cook for 10 minutes at 350 degrees F. Serve.

Nutrition Facts Per Serving

Calories 399, Carbohydrates 18g, Cholesterol 145mg, Total Fat 11g, Protein 57g, Sugar 13g, Fiber 0g, Sodium 232mg, Potassium 472mg

Conclusion

Thank you for downloading this book and reading it.

Every modern kitchen deserves the Instant Vortex air fryer. It can help you in so many ways. There are so many wonderful recipes to make.

I hope you have liked reading this book. I have tried to show you its many uses and benefits. Its time now to start preparing the recipes. Start with the ones you are comfortable with, and then maybe you can try a few new recipes.

Share the recipes with your friends and family. Better still, call them over, and show your cooking skills. Prepare food and eat together.

Happy cooking! Thank you and good luck!

CPSIA information can be obtained
at www.ICGtesting.com
Printed in the USA
LVHW061109051120
670808LV00018B/540

9 781952 832321